Getting R[...]
for the New Y[...]
Testing Program

Grade 2

Blackline Masters

INCLUDES:

- Prerequisite Skills Inventory
- Beginning-of-Year, Middle-of-Year, and End-of-Year Benchmark Tests
- Chapter Tests
- All Assessments in the Format of the New York State Testing Program
- Individual Record Forms
- Correlation to Standards

Contents

Tests and Management Forms

Overview of *GO Math!* Assessment

How Assessment Can Help Individualize Instruction

The *Getting Ready for the New York State Testing Program* contains several types of assessment for use throughout the school year. The following pages will explain how these assessments can be utilized to diagnose children's understanding of the New York State Mathematics Learning Standards and to guide instructional choices, improve children's performance, and help facilitate children's mastery of this year's objectives.

Diagnostic Assessment

Prerequisite Skills Inventory in the *Getting Ready for the New York State Testing Program* should be given at the beginning of the year or when a new child arrives. This short-answer test yields insight regarding understanding of prerequisite skills. Test results provide information about the review or intervention that children may need in order to be successful in the coming year. Suggestions for intervention are provided for this inventory.

Beginning-of-Year Test in the *Getting Ready for the New York State Testing Program* is a mixed-response format comprised of multiple-choice, short-answer, and extended constructed-response items. This test should be utilized early in the year to establish on-grade-level skills that children may already understand. This benchmark test will allow customization of instructional content to optimize the time spent teaching specific objectives. Suggestions for intervention are provided for this test.

Formative Assessment

Middle-of-Year Test in the *Getting Ready for the New York State Testing Program* assesses the same skills as the Beginning-of-Year Test, allowing monitoring of children's progress to permit instructional adjustments when required.

Summative Assessment

Chapter Test in the *Getting Ready for the New York State Testing Program* measures children's mastery of concepts and skills taught in the chapter. The test assesses the mastery of the New York State Mathematics Learning Standards taught in the chapter. It is a mixed-response-format test comprised of multiple-choice, short-answer, and extended constructed-response items.

Performance Tasks in the *Getting Ready for the New York State Testing Program* provide assessment of each grade level's Critical Areas. Each task assesses the children's ability to use what they have learned and provides an opportunity for children to display their thinking strategies. Correlations to the New York State Mathematics Learning Standards and performance indicators are provided. Use the associated rubric to score these assessments.

End-of-Year Test in the *Getting Ready for the New York State Testing Program* documents each child's level of mastery of the concepts and skills for the current grade level and mirrors the Beginning-and Middle-of-Year Tests. Used together, these mixed-response-format tests allow for monitoring of growth throughout the year.

© Houghton Mifflin Harcourt Publishing Company

New York State Testing Program Assessment Formats

The New York State Testing Program consists of assessments that contain mixed responses comprised of multiple-choice, short-answer, and extended constructed-response items. This allows for a more robust assessment of children's understanding of concepts. The New York State assessment is administered via several "books" and *GO Math!* presents items in formats similar to what children will see on the tests. The following information is provided to help teachers familiarize children with these different types of items. An example of each item type appears on the following pages. You may want to use the examples to introduce the item types to children. The following explanations are provided to guide children in answering the questions.

Example 1 Choose another representation of a given number.

Multiple Choice

For this type of item, children respond to a single question with several choices. There will be a question and children will choose the correct choice. It is important for children to know they must fill in the bubble to make their choice. There will only be one choice that is correct.

Example 2 Find a number less than a given number.

Short Answer

This type of item will ask them to solve a problem and show their work. The children will need to explain how they got their answers. They may need to make or complete a drawing to show their work. Tell them to think about their answers carefully. There are some questions that will have more than one correct answer.

Example 3 Solve and explain a problem with multiple parts.

Extended Constructed Response

This type of item will ask children to solve a problem that has two parts. The children will be expected to show their work. This can be shown with an explanation or with a drawing. Tell them to think about their answers carefully. There are some questions that will have more than one correct answer.

1. Which of these is a way to show 42?

   ○ 4 + 2   ○   ○ 40 + 20   ○

---

2. What is a number **less than** 25?

Show your work.

Answer _____

---

3. There are 3 frogs on the grass. More frogs are in the pond. There are 12 frogs in all.

PART A

How many frogs are in the pond?

Show your work.

Answer _____ frogs

PART B

How many **more** frogs are in the pond than on the grass? Write a subtraction sentence to solve the problem.

Show your work.

Answer _____ more frogs

1. Look at the model of 15.

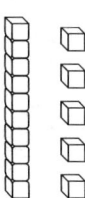

Write how many tens and ones are in the model.

_____ ten _____ ones

2. Write how many tens and ones are in 12.

_____ ten _____ ones

3. Draw tens and ones to show 13.

4. Circle a group of ten to show 1 ten and some ones.

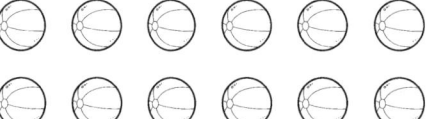

5. Write how many tens are the same as 10 ones.

10 ones = _____ ten

6. Compare using $<$, $>$, or $=$.

12 ◯ 15

GO ON ➤

7. Subtract.

$$15 - 8 = \underline{\hphantom{xxxx}}$$

8. Add.

$$8 + 2 + 6 = \underline{\hphantom{xxxx}}$$

9. Subtract.

$$18 - 9 = \underline{\hphantom{xxxx}}$$

10. Add.

$$6 + 4 + 7 = \underline{\hphantom{xxxx}}$$

11. If $5 + 6 = 11$, then

$$11 - \underline{\hphantom{xxxx}} = 6.$$

12. If $17 - 9 = 8$, then

$$\underline{\hphantom{xxxx}} + 9 = 17.$$

GO ON ▶

13.

$8 + 7 =$ _____

is the same as

$7 +$ _____ $+ 1 =$ _____

14.

$3 + 4 =$ _____

is the same as

$3 +$ _____ $+ 1 =$ _____

15. Add.

$9 + 1 + 7 =$ _____

16. $12 - 4 =$ ▢

is the same as

$12 -$ _____ $- 2 =$ ▢

So, $12 - 4 =$ _____.

17. Subtract.

$60 - 50 =$ _____

18. If $3 + 4 + 6 = 13$, then

$3 +$ _____ $= 13$.

GO ON ▶

19. Add.

$$\begin{array}{r} 66 \\ +9 \\ \hline \end{array}$$

☐

20. Add.

68 + 20 = _____

21. Write the time.

_____ : _____

22. Write the time.

_____ : _____

23. Draw hands to show 3:30 on the clock.

24. Use the bar graph.

Favorite Animal						
cats						
dogs						
rabbits						

Animals

0 1 2 3 4 5 6
Number of Children

How many children chose dogs?

_____ children

GO ON ▶

Use the picture graph for questions 25–26.

Children in the Class										
girls	�	☺	☺	☺	☺	☺				
boys	☺	☺	☺	☺	☺	☺	☺	☺	☺	☺

Each ☺ stands for 1 child.

25. How many children are in the class?

_____ children

26. How many fewer girls are there than boys?

_____ fewer girls

27. Use ■. About how long is the pencil?

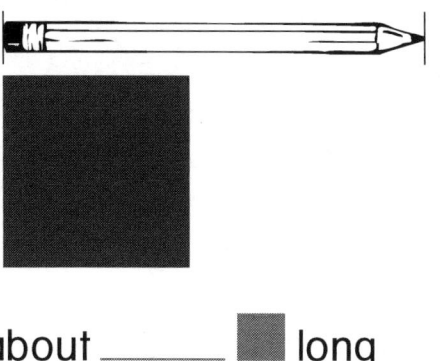

about _____ ■ long

28. Use ■. Draw a line that is about 3 ■ long.

29. Draw three lines in order from **longest** to **shortest**.

longest	
shortest	

GO ON ➡

30. A pencil is longer than a marker.
The marker is longer than a crayon.

Write **shorter** or **longer** to finish the sentence.

The pencil is _____ than the crayon.

---

31. Combine  and .
Circle the new shape you can make.

---

32. Use pattern blocks.
Draw to show the blocks.

How many make a

 ?

_____  make a  .

33. Write the number of
equal shares.

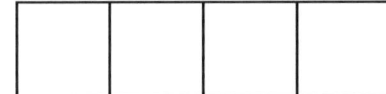

_____ equal shares

STOP

Choose the correct answer.

1. Which shows a related addition fact?

$$15 - 8 = 7$$

- ○ $15 + 7 = 22$
- ○ $8 - 7 = 1$
- ○ $7 + 8 = 15$
- ○ $23 - 8 = 15$

2. There are 9 bugs on the grass and 5 bugs on a leaf. Which number sentence shows how many bugs there are in all?

- ○ $10 + 5 = 15$
- ○ $9 + 5 = 14$
- ○ $9 - 5 = 4$
- ○ $5 + 4 = 9$

3. Gina has 4 green trains, 2 red trains, and 6 yellow trains. How many trains does Gina have in all?

- ○ 6
- ○ 8
- ○ 10
- ○ 12

4. There are 725 students in the school. There are 343 boys. How many girls are there?

Hundreds	Tens	Ones
☐	☐	☐
7	2	5
− 3	4	3

- ○ 382
- ○ 422
- ○ 428
- ○ 482

GO ON ➡

5. Chelsea's soccer team collected 427 cans for donation. Jordan's basketball team collected 378 cans. How many cans did the two teams collect?

○ 685   ○ 805

○ 713   ○ 937

6. What is the difference?

$$\begin{array}{r} 402 \\ -\ 173 \\ \hline \end{array}$$

○ 339   ○ 329

○ 331   ○ 229

7. Use an inch ruler. What is the length of the ribbon to the nearest inch?

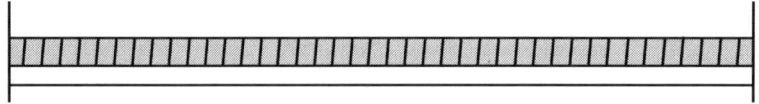

○ 8 inches   ○ 4 inches

○ 6 inches   ○ 2 inches

8. Glen made a line plot to show the lengths of his toy airplanes. How many planes are shown in the line plot?

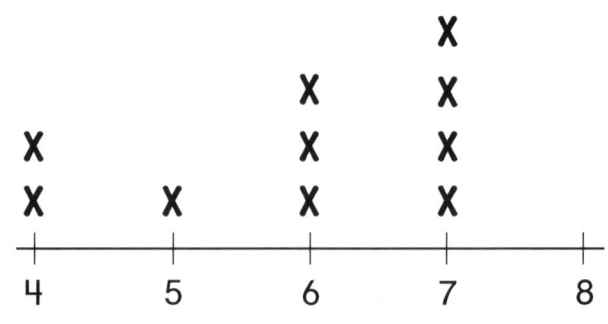

Lengths of Toy Airplanes in Inches

○ 7

○ 8

○ 9

○ 10

GO ON

9. Which is the **best** estimate of the length of a baseball bat?

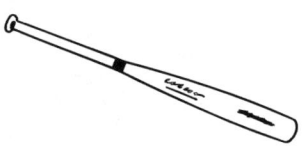

○ 2 feet

○ 6 feet

○ 8 feet

○ 10 feet

10. Fred wants to measure the distance around a ball. Which is the **best** tool for Fred to use?

○ counters

○ cup

○ measuring tape

○ pencil

11. Ms. Angeles writes an odd number on the board. Which could be the number that Ms. Angeles writes?

○ 3

○ 4

○ 6

○ 8

12. What is the value of the underlined digit?

3̲8

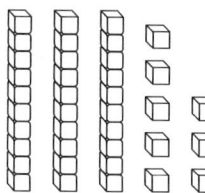

○ 3

○ 8

○ 30

○ 80

GO ON ➡

13. Which shows another way to write the number?

57

○ 7 tens 5 ones

○ fifty-seven

○ 5 + 70

○ 5 + 7

14. Kayleigh starts at 370 and counts by tens. What are the next 6 numbers Kayleigh will say?

○ 390, 410, 430, 450, 470, 490

○ 380, 390, 400, 410, 420, 430

○ 375, 385, 395, 405, 415, 425

○ 371, 372, 373, 374, 375, 376

15. Which object is shaped like a cylinder?

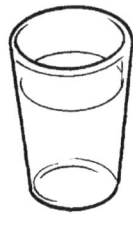

○

○

○

○

16. Danny makes a pentagon with straws. He uses one straw for each side of the shape. How many straws does Danny need?

○ 1

○ 3

○ 4

○ 5

GO ON

17. Which of these shapes has **fewer** than 4 angles?

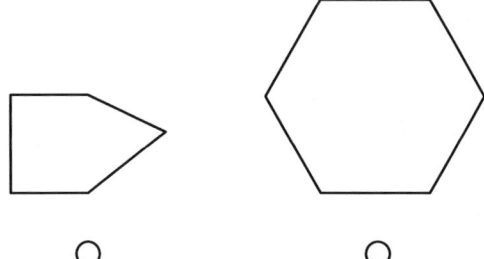

○   ○

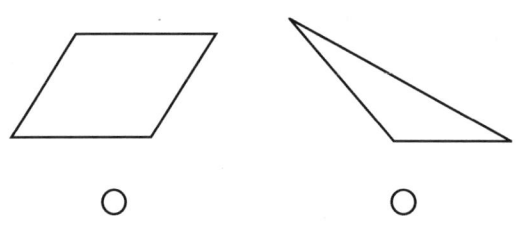

○   ○

18. Which shows a half of the shape shaded?

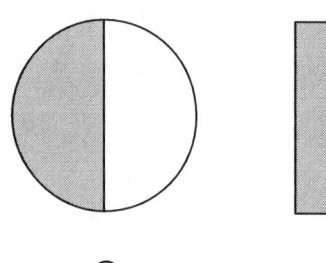

○   ○

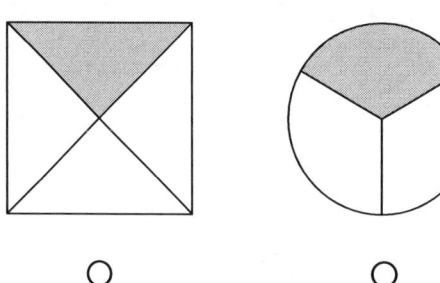

○   ○

19. A store sold 21 green rings and 38 red rings. Which number sentence tells how many rings the store sold?

○ $38 - 21 = 17$

○ $38 + 0 = 38$

○ $21 + 38 = 59$

○ $12 + 38 = 50$

20. What is the sum?

$$\begin{array}{r} 24 \\ 15 \\ + \ 36 \\ \hline \end{array}$$

○ 75

○ 65

○ 51

○ 39

GO ON ➡

21. Jared has 29 blocks. Amanda has 46 blocks. How many blocks do they have?

   ○ 75   ○ 83

   ○ 79   ○ 87

22. What is the sum?

$$\begin{array}{r} 75 \\ +\ 15 \\ \hline \end{array}$$

   ○ 60   ○ 85

   ○ 80   ○ 90

Use the picture graph for Questions 23–24.

Favorite Color					
blue	☺	☺	☺		
green	☺	☺			
red	☺	☺	☺	☺	☺

Key: Each ☺ stands for 1 child.

23. How many **more** children chose red than green?

   ○ 2   ○ 5

   ○ 3   ○ 7

24. 2 more children choose green. How many ☺ should be in the green row now?

   ○ 7   ○ 4

   ○ 5   ○ 3

GO ON ➡

25. Ian made a tally chart of the flowers he planted.

Flowers Planted	
Flower	**Tally**
roses	||||
daisies	ⅢⅡ |||
tulips	ⅢⅡ

How many tulips did Ian plant?

○ 4   ○ 6

○ 5   ○ 8

26. Use the bar graph.

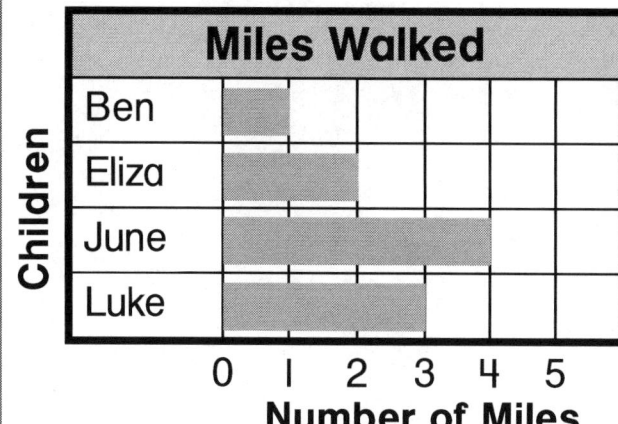

Who walked the **fewest** number of miles?

○ Ben   ○ June

○ Eliza   ○ Luke

27. Which number has the digit 4 in the hundreds place?

○ 42

○ 140

○ 453

○ 964

28. Which shows another way to write the number?

five hundred thirty-seven

○ 5 + 3 + 7

○ 50 + 37

○ 50 + 30 + 7

○ 500 + 30 + 7

GO ON ➡

29. Look at the pattern. What number comes next?

126, 136, 146, 156, ▨

○ 157 ○ 178

○ 166 ○ 256

30. Which comparison is **true**?

○ 542 > 621

○ 382 > 405

○ 261 < 243

○ 215 < 225

---

31. Melissa gave her brother these coins. What is the value of the coins?

30 cents   65 cents   80 cents   95 cents

○   ○   ○   ○

---

32. Lara wants to buy a marker that costs one dollar. Which coins have a total value of one dollar?

○ 100 dimes

○ 100 pennies

○ 10 pennies

○ 10 nickels

GO ON ➡

33. Jason went on a morning run
at the time shown on the clock.
At what time did Jason go for his run?

10:45 A.M.　　10:45 P.M.　　9:55 A.M.　　9:55 P.M.
　○　　　　　　○　　　　　　○　　　　　　○

---

34. Break apart the ones to subtract. What is the difference?

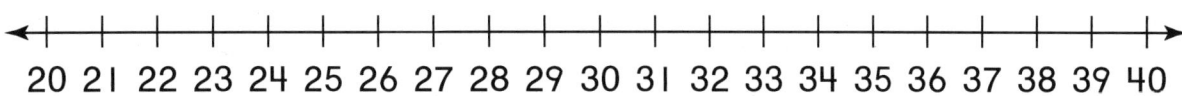

20 21 22 23 24 25 26 27 28 29 30 31 32 33 34 35 36 37 38 39 40

$$33 - 6 = \underline{\qquad}$$

30　　　　　　29　　　　　　28　　　　　　27
○　　　　　　○　　　　　　○　　　　　　○

---

35. Rita had 37 pencils. She gave
away 14 pencils. Which number
sentence can be used to find
how many pencils Rita has now?

○ $23 - \boxed{} = 14$

○ $30 + \boxed{} = 37$

○ $37 - 14 = \boxed{}$

○ $37 + 14 = \boxed{}$

36. Steven picks 22 berries. He
picks 18 more berries. Then
he eats 13 berries. How many
berries does Steven have now?

○ 5

○ 27

○ 37

○ 40

37. What is the difference?

$$80 \\ - \ 26$$

○ 4 tens 4 ones

○ 4 tens 6 ones

○ 5 tens 4 ones

○ 8 tens 2 ones

38. Which statement is **true?**

○ I centimeter is longer than I meter.

○ I meter is longer than I centimeter.

○ I meter is shorter than I centimeter.

○ I meter is the same as I centimeter.

39. Measure the length of the rope to the nearest centimeter. Which length is the **best** choice?

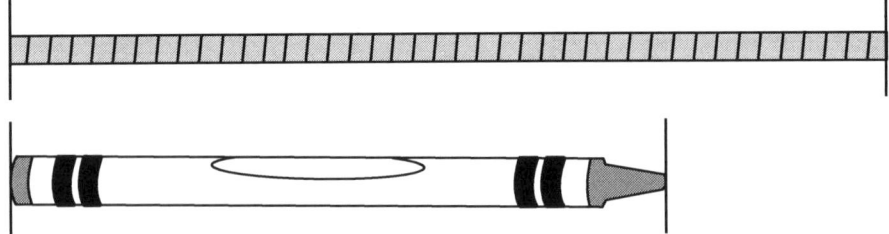

○ 5 centimeters   ○ I I centimeters

○ 8 centimeters   ○ I 3 centimeters

40. Use a centimeter ruler. Measure the length of each object.

How much longer is the ribbon than the crayon?

○ 2 I centimeters longer   ○ 9 centimeters longer

○ I 2 centimeters longer   ○ 3 centimeters longer

41. Write an odd number between 5 and 15.
Draw a picture, and then write a sentence to
explain why it is an odd number.

Show your work.

Answer _____

_____

---

42. Kendall uses 7 crayons to color her picture.
She has 11 crayons in all. How many crayons
does Kendall **not** use? Draw a picture to show
the two groups of crayons.

Show your work.

Answer _____ crayons

43. Describe how you would solve the following problem. Fill in the missing numbers.

$$189$$
$$+ \ 24\_$$
$$\overline{\quad \_3}$$

Answer _____

_____

_____

_____

---

44. Allen asked some friends to name their favorite color.

2 children like red.

5 children like blue.

3 children like green.

I child likes yellow.

PART A

Complete the bar graph

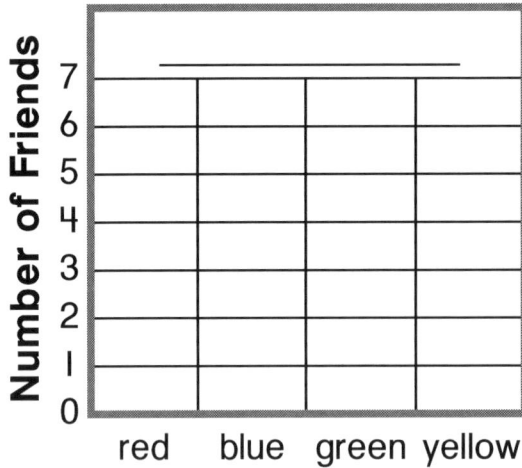

_____

PART B

Which color was the **most** popular? Explain.

Answer _____ STOP

Choose the correct answer.

1. Which shows a related subtraction fact?

$$9 + 5 = 14$$

○ $19 - 14 = 5$

○ $14 + 5 = 19$

○ $14 - 5 = 9$

○ $9 - 5 = 4$

2. There were 16 birds at the park. Then 9 birds flew away. Which number sentence shows how many birds are at the park now?

○ $16 + 9 = 25$

○ $16 - 9 = 7$

○ $9 - 7 = 2$

○ $2 + 7 = 9$

3. Fran picks 3 red flowers, 7 yellow flowers, and 3 pink flowers. How many flowers does Fran pick in all?

○ 6

○ 10

○ 12

○ 13

4. There are 429 students at the museum. There are 180 boys. How many girls are at the museum?

Hundreds	Tens	Ones
☐	☐	☐
4	2	9
− 1	8	0

○ 239

○ 249

○ 349

○ 369

GO ON ➤

5. Rhonda collected 256 shells to make necklaces. Jan collected 315 shells. How many shells did the two girls collect?

○ 476   ○ 571

○ 561   ○ 601

6. What is the difference?

$$507 - 368$$

○ 139   ○ 239

○ 149   ○ 241

7. Use an inch ruler. What is the length of the pencil to the nearest inch?

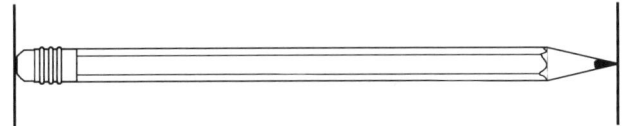

○ 5 inches   ○ 3 inches

○ 4 inches   ○ 2 inches

8. Larry made a line plot to show the lengths of his toy cars. How many cars are shown in the line plot?

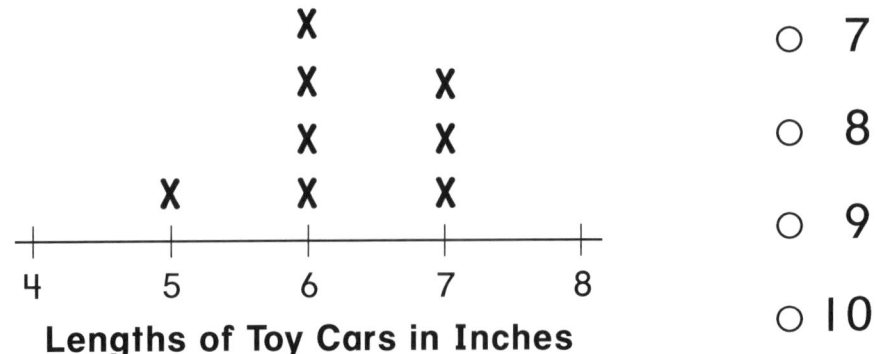

Lengths of Toy Cars in Inches

○ 7

○ 8

○ 9

○ 10

GO ON

9. Which is the **best** estimate of the length of a real park bench?

○   1 foot

○   6 feet

○ 15 feet

○ 20 feet

10. Frank wants to measure the length of a bus. Which is the **best** tool for Frank to use?

○ yardstick

○ counters

○ cup

○ pencil

11. Ms. Ikeda writes an even number on the board. Which could be the number that Ms. Ikeda writes?

○   7

○ 11

○ 13

○ 14

12. What is the value of the underlined digit?

45

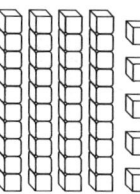

○ 50   ○ 5

○ 40   ○ 4

GO ON ➡

13. Which shows another way to write the number?

32

○ 3 tens 2 ones

○ twenty-three

○ 20 + 3

○ 3 + 2

14. Vanessa starts at 460 and counts by tens. What are the next 6 numbers Vanessa will say?

○ 470, 480, 490, 500, 510, 520

○ 465, 470, 475, 480, 485, 490

○ 462, 464, 466, 468, 470, 472

○ 461, 462, 463, 464, 465, 466

15. Which object is shaped like a cone?

○

○

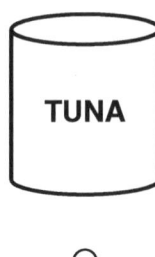

TUNA

○

○

16. Danny makes a triangle with straws. He uses one straw for each side of the shape. How many straws does Danny need?

○ 3

○ 4

○ 5

○ 6

GO ON ➡

17. Which of these shapes has **fewer** than 5 angles?

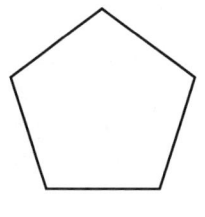 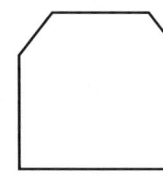

○　　　　　　　○

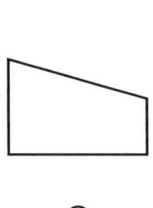 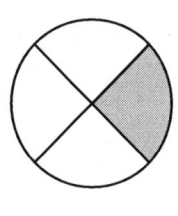

○　　　　　　　○

18. Which shows a third of the shape shaded?

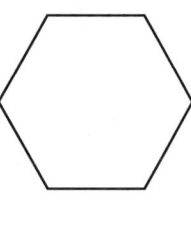 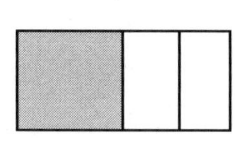

○　　　　　　　○

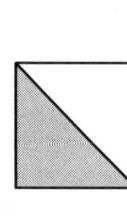 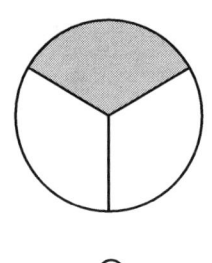

○　　　　　　　○

19. Beth has 26 stickers. Ken has 51 stickers. Which number sentence tells how many stickers Beth and Ken have?

○ 51 − 26 = 25

○ 26 + 51 = 77

○ 26 + 25 = 51

○ 15 + 26 = 41

20. What is the sum?

$$\begin{array}{r} 18 \\ 32 \\ +\ 12 \\ \hline \end{array}$$

○ 62

○ 52

○ 50

○ 44

GO ON ▶

21. Jacob has 46 marbles. Chloe has 31 marbles. How many marbles do they have?

○ 65   ○ 79

○ 77   ○ 81

22. What is the sum?

$$\begin{array}{r} 57 \\ +\ 14 \\ \hline \end{array}$$

○ 43   ○ 63

○ 61   ○ 71

Use the picture graph for Questions 23–24.

Favorite Muffin					
berry	☺	☺	☺		
corn	☺	☺	☺	☺	☺
pumpkin	☺				

Key: Each ☺ stands for 1 child.

23. How many **more** children chose berry than pumpkin?

○ 1   ○ 3

○ 2   ○ 5

24. **2 more** children choose pumpkin. How many ☺ should be in the pumpkin row now?

○ 3   ○ 5

○ 4   ○ 7

GO ON ➡

25. Julio made a tally chart of the vegetables he planted.

Vegetables Planted	
Vegetable	**Tally**
beans	⩗ I
carrots	IIII
peas	⩗ II

How many peas did Julio plant?

○ 4   ○ 7

○ 6   ○ 10

26. Use the bar graph.

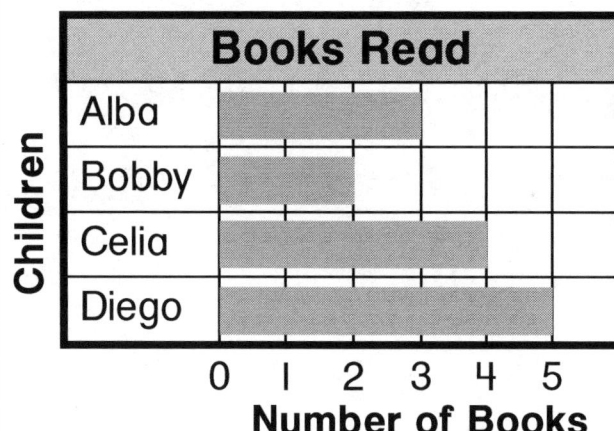

Who read the **most** books?

○ Alba   ○ Celia

○ Bobby   ○ Diego

27. Which number has the digit 8 in the tens place?

○ 8,000

○ 586

○ 298

○ 803

28. Which shows another way to write the number?

seven hundred thirteen

○   7 + 13

○ 70 + 13

○ 70 + 10 + 3

○ 700 + 10 + 3

GO ON ▶

29. Look at the pattern. What number comes next?

218, 318, 418, 518, ▓

○ 519   ○ 600

○ 528   ○ 618

30. Which comparison is true?

○ 253 > 315

○ 315 > 381

○ 354 < 366

○ 472 < 425

---

31. Melinda gave her friend these coins. What is the value of the coins?

45 cents   55 cents   60 cents   75 cents
   ○   ○   ○   ○

---

32. Clara wants to buy a comb that costs one dollar. Which coins have a total value of one dollar?

○ 20 dimes

○ 20 nickels

○ 5 dimes

○ 5 nickels

33. Jared ate lunch at the time shown on the clock. At what time did Jared eat lunch?

12:15 A.M.   12:15 P.M.   3:00 A.M.   3:00 P.M.
   ○   ○   ○   ○

---

34. Break apart the ones to subtract. What is the difference?

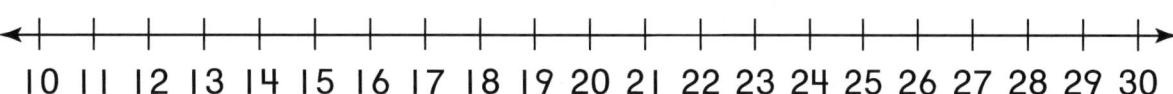

10 11 12 13 14 15 16 17 18 19 20 21 22 23 24 25 26 27 28 29 30

$$24 - 6 = \underline{\hspace{1cm}}$$

20   19   18   17
○   ○   ○   ○

---

35. Ana has 36 cups. She fills 12 cups with juice. Which number sentence can be used to find how many cups are empty?

○ $12 + \boxed{} = 30$

○ $24 - \boxed{} = 12$

○ $36 + 12 = \boxed{}$

○ $36 - 12 = \boxed{}$

36. Mark has 59 shells. He gives 21 shells to Ethan and 16 shells to Beth. How many shells does Mark have now?

○ 22

○ 37

○ 38

○ 43

37. What is the difference?

$$\begin{array}{r} 90 \\ - \ 38 \\ \hline \end{array}$$

○ 6 tens 8 ones

○ 6 tens 2 ones

○ 5 tens 8 ones

○ 5 tens 2 ones

38. Which statement is **true?**

○ I meter is the same as
   I centimeter.

○ I meter is shorter than
   I centimeter.

○ I centimeter is longer than
   I meter.

○ I centimeter is shorter than
   I meter.

39. Measure the length of the rope to the nearest centimeter. Which length is the best choice?

○ 6 centimeters   ○ 10 centimeters

○ 8 centimeters   ○ 12 centimeters

40. Use a centimeter ruler. Measure the length of each object.

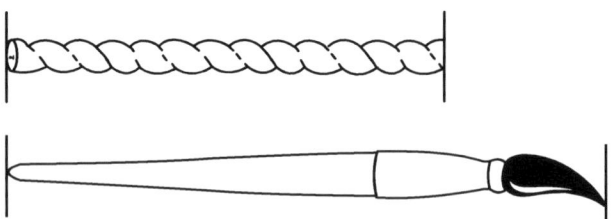

How much longer is the paintbrush than the string?

○ 16 centimeters longer   ○ 6 centimeters longer

○ 10 centimeters longer   ○ 2 centimeters longer

41. Write an even number between 8 and 16.
Draw a picture, and then write a sentence
to explain why it is an even number.

Show your work.

Answer _____
_____

42. Veronica uses 5 colors of paint to color her picture.
She has 12 colors in all. How many colors of
paint does Veronica **not** use? Draw a picture to show
the two groups of colors.

Show your work.

Answer _____ colors

43. Describe how you would solve the following problem. Fill in the
missing numbers.

$$
\begin{array}{r}
278 \\
+\ 35\_ \\
\hline
\_2
\end{array}
$$

Answer _____
_____
_____
_____

44. Patricia asked some friends to name their favorite animal.

4 children like cats.

5 children like horses.

6 children like dogs.

2 children like gerbils.

PART A

Complete the bar graph.

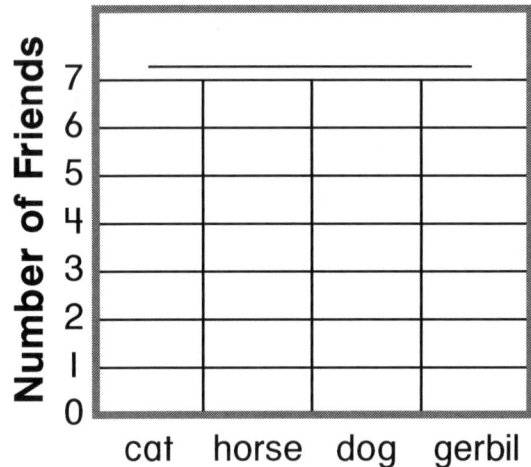

PART B

Which animal was the **most** popular? Explain.

Answer _____

Choose the correct answer.

1. Which shows a related addition fact?

$$17 - 9 = 8$$

- ○ $17 + 9 = 26$
- ○ $9 - 8 = 1$
- ○ $8 + 9 = 17$
- ○ $25 - 8 = 17$

2. There are 7 big dogs and 6 small dogs. Which number sentence shows how many dogs there are in all?

- ○ $7 + 6 = 13$
- ○ $7 - 1 = 6$
- ○ $10 + 7 = 17$
- ○ $19 - 7 = 12$

3. Tess collects 2 green leaves, 8 red leaves, and 5 yellow leaves. How many leaves does Tess collect in all?

- ○ 7
- ○ 10
- ○ 13
- ○ 15

4. There are 545 seats at the theater. 362 seats are filled. How many seats are empty?

Hundreds	Tens	Ones
☐	☐	☐
5	4	5
− 3	6	2

- ○ 283
- ○ 223
- ○ 183
- ○ 123

GO ON ▶

5. Josh collected 233 baseball cards for his collection. Dave collected 428 cards. How many cards did the two boys collect?

○ 396   ○ 551

○ 435   ○ 661

6. What is the difference?

$$803$$
$$- \; 427$$

○ 486   ○ 386

○ 476   ○ 376

7. Use an inch ruler. What is the length of the paintbrush to the nearest inch?

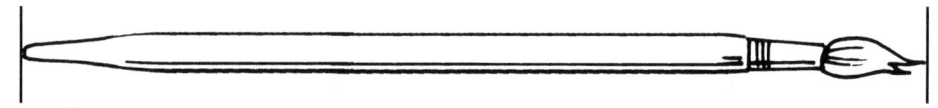

○ 4 inches   ○ 6 inches

○ 5 inches   ○ 7 inches

8. Billy made a line plot to show the lengths of his toy trains. How many trains are shown in the line plot?

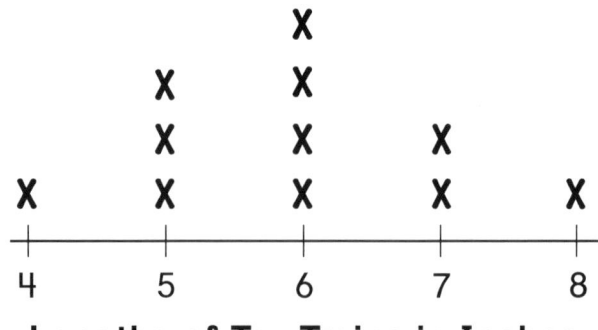

Lengths of Toy Trains in Inches

○ 9

○ 10

○ 11

○ 12

GO ON

9. Which is the **best** estimate of the length of an adult's shoe?

○ 1 foot

○ 3 feet

○ 5 feet

○ 9 feet

10. Eddie wants to measure the distance around a water bottle. Which is the **best** tool for Eddie to use?

○ cup

○ measuring tape

○ pencil

○ counters

11. Ms. Martinez writes an even number on the board. Which could be the number that Ms. Martinez writes?

○ 13

○ 11

○ 10

○ 9

12. What is the value of the underlined digit?

<u>6</u>2

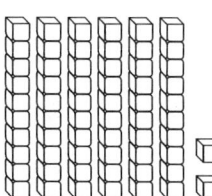

○ 2   ○ 20

○ 6   ○ 60

GO ON

13. Which shows another way to write the number?

74

○ 4 tens 7 ones

○ forty-seven

○ 70 + 4

○ 7 + 4

14. Kelly starts at 180 and counts by tens. What are the next 6 numbers Kelly will say?

○ 181, 182, 183, 184, 185, 186

○ 182, 184, 186, 188, 190, 192

○ 185, 190, 195, 200, 205, 210

○ 190, 200, 210, 220, 230, 240

15. Which object is shaped like a cube?

   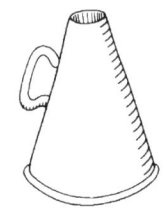

○   ○

○   ○

16. Danny makes a hexagon with straws. He uses one straw for each side of the shape. How many straws does Danny need?

○ 3

○ 4

○ 5

○ 6

GO ON

17. Which of these shapes has **more** than 5 sides?

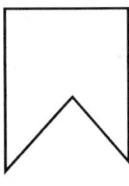 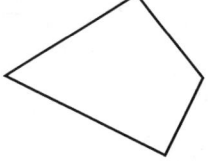

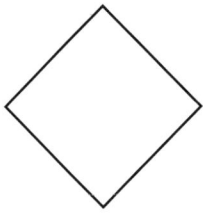 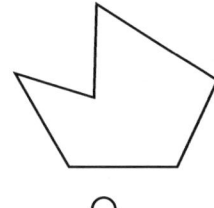

18. Which shows a fourth of the shape shaded?

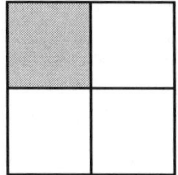 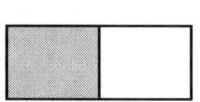

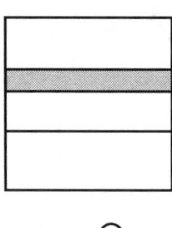 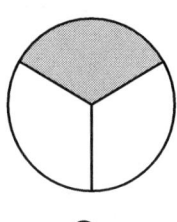

19. Jen has 52 beads. She buys 17 more beads. Which number sentence tells how many beads Jen has now?

○ $52 + 17 = 69$

○ $52 - 17 = 35$

○ $35 + 17 = 52$

○ $25 + 17 = 42$

20. What is the sum?

$$
\begin{array}{r}
43 \\
27 \\
+\ 13 \\
\hline
\end{array}
$$

○ 40

○ 70

○ 73

○ 83

GO ON

21. Anne has 34 crayons. Carey has 14 crayons. How many crayons do they have?

○ 20   ○ 50

○ 48   ○ 68

22. What is the sum?

$$38$$
$$+\ 23$$

○ 15   ○ 55

○ 51   ○ 61

Use the picture graph for Questions 23–24.

Favorite Meal					
breakfast	☺	☺			
lunch	☺	☺	☺		
dinner	☺	☺	☺	☺	☺

Key: Each ☺ stands for 1 child.

23. How many **more** children chose dinner than breakfast?

○ 1   ○ 3

○ 2   ○ 5

24. **2 more** children choose lunch. How many ☺ should be in the lunch row now?

○ 2   ○ 5

○ 4   ○ 7

GO ON ➤

25. Mr. Campa made a tally chart of the trees he sold.

Trees Sold	
Tree	**Tally**
apple	卌 IIII
oak	III
pine	卌 I

How many pine trees did Mr. Campa sell?

○ 3   ○ 9

○ 6   ○ 10

26. Use the bar graph.

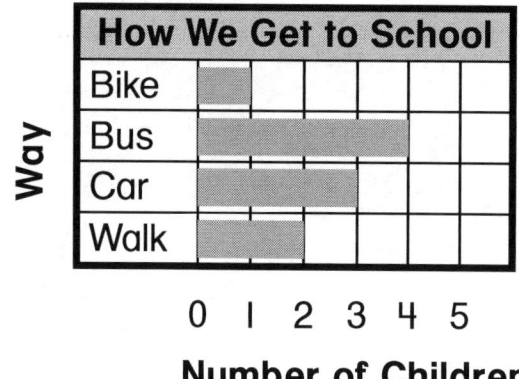

How many children do **not** take the bus to school?

○ 6   ○ 2

○ 3   ○ 1

27. Which number has the digit 2 in the hundreds place?

○ 2,000

○ 742

○ 298

○ 25

28. Which shows another way to write the number?

four hundred twenty-three

○ 4 + 2 + 3

○ 40 + 23

○ 400 + 20 + 3

○ 400 + 20 + 30

GO ON

29. Look at the pattern. What number comes next?

351, 361, 371, 381, ▢

○ 382   ○ 391

○ 386   ○ 481

30. Which comparison is **true**?

○ 323 > 304

○ 295 > 405

○ 215 < 154

○ 165 < 123

---

31. Steve gave his sister these coins. What is the value of the coins?

65 cents   75 cents   80 cents   90 cents

○   ○   ○   ○

---

32. Hugo wants to buy a bottle of juice that costs one dollar. Which coins have a total value of one dollar?

○ 10 quarters

○ 10 nickels

○ 4 quarters

○ 4 nickels

33. Emily went to bed for the night at the time shown on the clock. At what time did Emily go to bed?

5:40 A.M.   5:40 P.M.   8:25 A.M.   8:25 P.M.
   ○   ○   ○   ○

---

34. Break apart the ones to subtract. What is the difference?

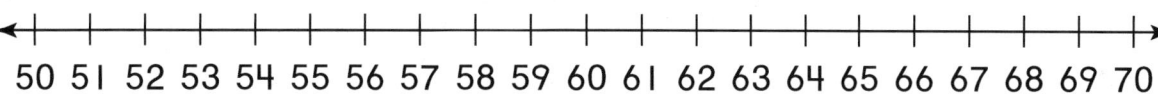

50 51 52 53 54 55 56 57 58 59 60 61 62 63 64 65 66 67 68 69 70

$$62 - 6 = \underline{\qquad}$$

68   60   58   56
○   ○   ○   ○

---

35. Mia had 48 stickers. She gave away 17 stickers. Which number sentence can be used to find how many stickers Mia has now?

○ $40 + \square = 48$

○ $48 - 17 = \square$

○ $48 + 17 = \square$

○ $65 - \square = 48$

36. Jamal has a box with 35 crayons. He puts 22 more crayons in the box. Then he takes 14 crayons out of the box. How many crayons are in the box now?

○ 57

○ 53

○ 43

○ 8

GO ON

37. What is the difference?

$$70$$
$$- 44$$

○ 2 tens 4 ones

○ 2 tens 6 ones

○ 3 tens 4 ones

○ 3 tens 6 ones

38. Which statement is **true?**

○ I meter is longer than
   I centimeter.

○ I meter is shorter than
   I centimeter.

○ I centimeter is the same
   as I meter.

○ I centimeter is longer than
   I meter.

39. Measure the length of the rope to the nearest centimeter. Which length is the **best** choice?

○ 6 centimeters   ○ 9 centimeters

○ 8 centimeters   ○ I I centimeters

40. Use a centimeter ruler. Measure the length of each object.

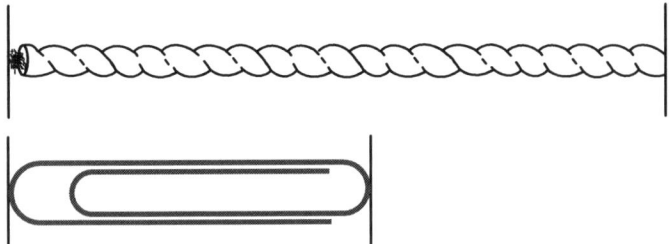

How much longer is the string than the paperclip?

○ I4 centimeters longer   ○ 5 centimeters longer

○ 9 centimeters longer   ○ 4 centimeters longer 

41. Write an odd number between 2 and 9.
Draw a picture, and then write a sentence to
explain why it is an odd number.

Show your work.

Answer _____
_____

42. Sarah uses 8 colored pencils to color her picture.
She has 15 colored pencils in all. How many
colored pencils does Sarah **not** use? Draw a picture
to show the two groups of colored pencils.

Show your work.

Answer _____ colored pencils

43. Describe how you would solve the following problem. Fill in the
missing numbers.

$$
\begin{array}{r}
367 \\
+\ 27\underline{} \\
\hline
\underline{}4
\end{array}
$$

Answer _____
_____
_____
_____

44. Brooke asked some friends to name their favorite food to eat at a baseball game.

3 children like peanuts.

2 children like popcorn.

4 children like hamburgers.

5 children like hot dogs.

PART A

Complete the bar graph.

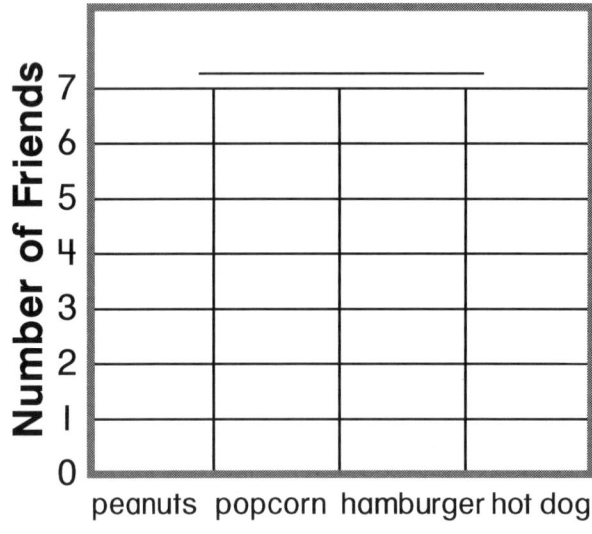

PART B

Which food was the **most** popular? Explain.

Answer _____

Choose the correct answer.

1. Which shows $7 + 7 = 14$?

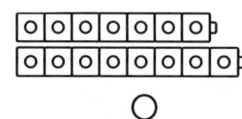

○   ○

○   ○

2. Which sum is an even number?

○ $4 + 5 = 9$

○ $4 + 4 = 8$

○ $3 + 4 = 7$

○ $4 + 1 = 5$

3. Paul counts by twos to 20.

Karen counts by ones to 10.

Maria counts by fives to 50.

Who will say **more** numbers?

○ Paul

○ Karen

○ Maria

○ They all say the same amount.

4. Which of the numbers shows counting by fives?

○ 1, 5, 9, 13, 17

○ 5, 7, 9, 11, 13

○ 10, 20, 30, 40, 50

○ 15, 20, 25, 30, 35

GO ON ➤

5. Which is another way to describe 27?

○ 20 + 7

○ 20 + 70

○ 2 + 7

○ 70 + 2

6. Which is another way to describe 52?

○ 5 + 2

○ 20 + 5

○ 50 + 2

○ 500 + 2

7. Which shows how many tens and ones in 65?

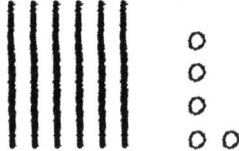

○ 5 tens 6 ones

○ 6 tens 0 ones

○ 6 tens 5 ones

○ 6 tens 6 ones

8. Which is another way to write thirty-eight?

○   8

○   38

○   83

○ 308

GO ON ▶

9. Which is another way to write sixty-four?

○ 64 + 4

○ 4 tens 6 ones

○ 60 + 40

○ 64

10. Which is another way to write the number?

10 + 6

○ 16

○ 26

○ 61

○ 66

11. Count by tens.

435, 445, 455, 465, _____

What number comes next?

○ 565

○ 475

○ 470

○ 466

12. Which group of numbers shows counting by hundreds?

○ 100, 105, 110, 115

○ 200, 201, 202, 203

○ 300, 400, 500, 600

○ 400, 410, 420, 430

GO ON

13. Ms. Brice buys 37 markers for the classroom. What choice is missing from the list?

Packs of 10 markers	Single markers
3	7
2	17
0	37

○ 3 packs, 7 markers

○ 1 pack, 27 markers

○ 1 pack, 17 markers

○ 0 packs, 27 markers

14. Ann needs 12 folders for school. What choice is missing from the list?

Packs of 10 folders	Single folders
0	12

○ 2 packs, 0 folders

○ 2 packs, 1 folder

○ 1 pack, 12 folders

○ 1 pack, 2 folders

15. Jon wants to buy 21 apples. What choice is missing from the list?

Bags of 10 apples	Single apples
2	1
1	11

○ 0 bags, 21 apples

○ 0 bags, 11 apples

○ 1 bag, 21 apples

○ 2 bags, 2 apples

16. The blocks show the number 30. Which is a way to show this number?

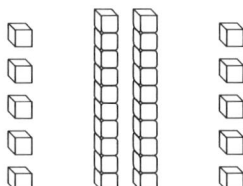

○ 1 ten 5 ones

○ 1 ten 10 ones

○ 2 tens 5 ones

○ 2 tens 10 ones

GO ON

17. Cameron is thinking of a number that has a digit that is **less than** 4 in the tens place. It has a digit **greater than** 6 in the ones place. What could Cameron's number be?

○ 88

○ 60 + 9

○ thirty-seven

○ five tens 4 ones

18. Which is a way to show the number 56?

○ 4 tens 6 ones

○ 4 tens 16 ones

○ 5 tens 16 ones

○ 5 tens 26 ones

19. Which ten frame shows an even number?

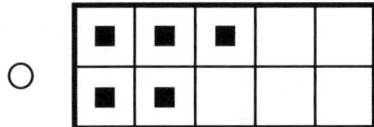

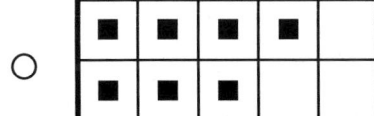

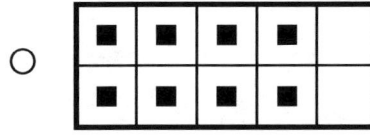

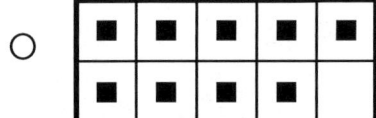

20. The Morris family has an even number of dogs and an odd number of cats. Which could be the number of pets in the Morris family?

○ 1 dog and 2 cats

○ 1 dog and 3 cats

○ 2 dogs and 1 cat

○ 2 dogs and 2 cats

GO ON

21. Katherine has an even number of bracelets and an odd number of necklaces. Which group of bracelets and necklaces could belong to Katherine?

○ 4 bracelets and 5 necklaces

○ 3 bracelets and 2 necklaces

○ 4 bracelets and 6 necklaces

○ 3 bracelets and 5 necklaces

22. Ally wrote this riddle:

My number has 9 tens and 1 one.

Which number matches Ally's clues?

○ 9

○ 11

○ 19

○ 91

23. What is the value of the digit 3 in 53?

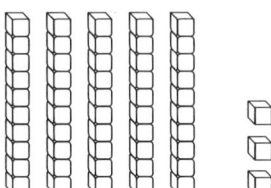

○ 30

○ 5

○ 3

○ 1

24. What is the value of the underlined digit?

27

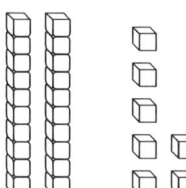

○ 2

○ 7

○ 20

○ 70

GO ON

25. Write an even number between 6 and 14. Draw a ten frame. Explain why it is an even number.

Show your work.

Answer _____

_____

26. Draw a picture to show the number 45. Describe the number in two ways.

Show your work.

Answer _____

GO ON

27. Amy starts at 190 and counts by tens. Find the next 6 numbers. Write the last number in two different ways.

Show your work.

Answer _____

---

28. Mr. Arnold needs 24 pencils. He can buy them in packs of 10 pencils or as single pencils.

PART A

Complete the chart to find all the different ways Mr. Arnold can buy the pencils.

Packs of 10 pencils	Single pencils

PART B

Choose two of the ways and explain how these ways show the same number of pencils.

Answer _____

_____

Name _____

Choose the correct answer.

1. Look at the picture. Which has the same value as 12 tens?

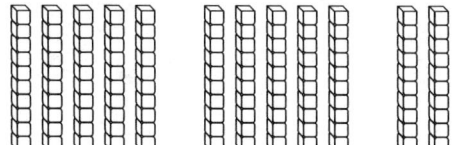

○ 2 tens

○ 2 hundreds

○ 1 hundred 1 ten

○ 1 hundred 2 tens

2. Sonya has 140 beads. How many bags of 10 beads does she need so that she will have 200 beads in all?

○ 6

○ 14

○ 20

○ 60

3. What is **10 more than** 529?

○ 429

○ 519

○ 539

○ 629

4. A store has 263 board games. It has **100 fewer** puzzles than board games. The store has **10 more** action figures than puzzles. How many action figures does it have?

○ 163

○ 173

○ 273

○ 353

5. Count the hundreds, tens, and ones. Which shows the same number?

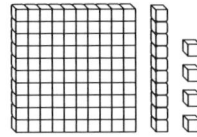

○ $400 + 40 + 1$

○ $400 + 10 + 4$

○ $100 + 40 + 1$

○ $100 + 10 + 4$

6. Ray sold 362 tickets to the show. Which is another way to write the number?

○ 6 hundreds 3 tens 2 ones

○ 3 hundreds 6 tens 3 ones

○ 3 hundreds 6 tens 2 ones

○ 2 hundreds 6 tens 3 ones

7. Sue's box has 264 pens. Which of these numbers is greater than 264?

○ 258

○ 246

○ 310

○ 188

8. Dana has 562 paper clips. Mitchell has fewer paper clips than Dana. Which number tells how many paper clips Mitchell could have?

○ 526

○ 563

○ 661

○ 572

9. Which number has the digit 6 in the hundreds place?

○ 68

○ 196

○ 362

○ 610

10. There are 203 birds in a zoo. What is the value of the digit 3 in the number 203?

○ 3

○ 30

○ 200

○ 300

11. Claudia's collection has four hundred sixty-five stickers. Which is another way to write the number?

○ 400 + 60 + 5

○ 400 + 600 + 5

○ 40 + 60 + 5

○ 4 + 6 + 5

12. Ollie draws a quick picture.

Which is another way to write Ollie's number?

○ 1 hundred 4 tens 8 ones

○ 100 + 8 + 4

○ 1 hundred 8 tens 4 ones

○ 100 + 80 + 7

13. How many hundreds does the picture show?

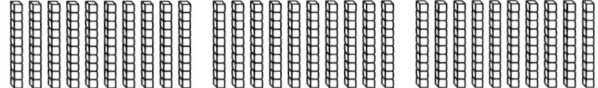

- ○ 30 hundreds

- ○ 20 hundreds

- ○ 3 hundreds

- ○ 2 hundreds

14. Which number has the same value as 80 tens?

- ○ 8

- ○ 80

- ○ 800

- ○ 801

15. What number is shown with these blocks?

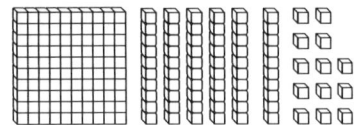

- ○ 133

- ○ 136

- ○ 163

- ○ 173

16. Rafi made this model of 309.

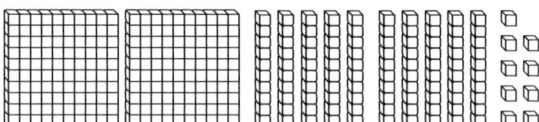

Which shows how many hundreds, tens, and ones?

○
Hundreds	Tens	Ones
3	19	0

○
Hundreds	Tens	Ones
3	10	9

○
Hundreds	Tens	Ones
2	0	19

○
Hundreds	Tens	Ones
2	10	9

GO ON ➡

17. What is the next number in the counting pattern?

472, 572, 672, 772

○ 773

○ 782

○ 872

○ 873

18. Rico wrote this counting pattern. What two numbers are next in Rico's pattern?

183, 283, 383, 483

○ 484, 485

○ 493, 503

○ 583, 683

○ 683, 783

19. Terry has 164 marbles. Which is another way to write the number 164?

○ one hundred sixteen

○ one hundred forty-six

○ one hundred sixty-four

○ four hundred sixty-one

20. There are two hundred four students in Marcy's school. Which shows this number?

○ 24

○ 204

○ 214

○ 240

21. Compare the numbers. Which symbol makes the comparison **true**?

241 214

○ >

○ <

○ =

○ +

22. Which of the following comparisons is **true**?

○ 120 < 115

○ 343 < 328

○ 691 > 706

○ 705 > 609

23. What number is shown with these blocks?

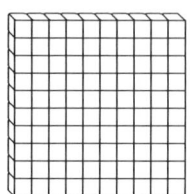

○ 12

○ 102

○ 120

○ 201

24. A store sells 2 boxes of 100 pencils and some single pencils. Which number shows how many pencils the store could sell?

○ 120

○ 182

○ 200

○ 206

GO ON

25. Sally needs 300 stickers. Vince gives her
12 packs with 10 stickers in each pack.
How many stickers does Sally need now?
Draw a picture to explain your answer.

Show your work.

Answer _____ stickers

---

26. Straws are sold in boxes, in bags, or as
single straws. Each box has 10 bags in it.
Each bag has 10 straws in it. Mr. Tan needs
355 straws. How many boxes, bags, and
single straws could he buy? Draw a picture
to explain your answer.

Show your work.

Answer _____ boxes, _____ bags and _____ straws

27. There are 154 days until Jeff's birthday. What are two ways the
number of days can be shown? Draw a picture to explain your answer.

Show your work.

Answer _____

---

28. Jill and Ed collect postcards. Jill has 124 postcards. Ed has
131 postcards.

PART A

Who has more postcards?

Answer _____

PART B

Jill gets 10 more postcards. Ed gets 5 more postcards. Who has
more postcards now?

Show your work.

Answer _____

Choose the correct answer.

1. What is the sum?

$$5 + 2$$

○ 4

○ 5

○ 6

○ 7

2. What is the difference?

$$13 - 9$$

○ 4

○ 5

○ 6

○ 7

3. Which number sentence has the same difference as $15 - 8 = \blacksquare$?

○ $10 - 1 = \blacksquare$

○ $10 - 2 = \blacksquare$

○ $10 - 3 = \blacksquare$

○ $10 - 4 = \blacksquare$

4. Which doubles fact could you use to find the sum of $4 + 5$?

○ $1 + 1$

○ $2 + 2$

○ $3 + 3$

○ $4 + 4$

GO ON ▶

5. Owen puts 4 apples in each basket. There are 6 baskets. How many apples are there in all?

○ 16

○ 20

○ 24

○ 28

6. Which shows a way to find the sum?

$$4 + 8 = \underline{\hspace{1cm}}$$

○ $10 + 2 = 12$

○ $10 + 4 = 14$

○ $10 + 6 = 16$

○ $10 + 8 = 18$

7. Ava grows 3 red flowers, 4 yellow flowers, and 4 purple flowers in her garden. How many flowers does Ava grow in all?

○ 7

○ 8

○ 10

○ 11

8. What is the sum?

$$4 + 5 + 7 = \underline{\hspace{1cm}}$$

○ 9

○ 11

○ 16

○ 17

GO ON

9. John has 16 rocks. He gives 7 rocks to his cousin. How many rocks does John have now?

○ 7

○ 8

○ 9

○ 10

10. What is the missing number in the related subtraction fact?

$$9 + 3 = 12$$

$$12 - 9 = \boxed{}$$

○ 9

○ 6

○ 4

○ 3

11. Eli has 13 marbles. Amber has 6 marbles. How many **more** marbles does Eli have than Amber?

○ 7

○ 8

○ 10

○ 19

12. Look at the picture. Which addition sentence shows the total number of shapes?

○ $3 + 5 = 8$

○ $3 + 3 + 3 = 9$

○ $5 + 5 + 5 = 15$

○ $5 + 5 + 5 + 5 + 5 = 25$

GO ON

13. David has 7 pencils in his pencil case. He has 1 pencil in his desk. How many pencils does David have?

○ 6

○ 7

○ 8

○ 9

14. Bob has 15 markers and 7 crayons. How many more markers than crayons does Bob have?

○ 7

○ 8

○ 12

○ 15

15. There are 11 books on a shelf. Then Reba takes some books off the shelf. Now there are 4 books on the shelf. How many books did Reba take off the shelf?

○ 15

○ 10

○ 8

○ 7

16. Peter sees 8 dogs. Beth sees 1 more dog than Peter. How many dogs do they see in all?

○ 18

○ 17

○ 16

○ 14

GO ON

17. Mia puts 5 crackers on each plate. How many crackers does she put on 3 plates?

○ 10

○ 15

○ 20

○ 25

18. There are 8 large plates and 7 small plates on a table. How many plates are on the table?

○ 10

○ 12

○ 15

○ 16

19. Kate sees 4 white dogs, 9 brown dogs, and 6 black dogs at the park. How many dogs does she see at the park?

○ 10

○ 15

○ 16

○ 19

20. Mark picks 11 apples. Anna picks 5 apples. Which number sentence shows how many **fewer** apples Anna picked than Mark?

○ $16 - 11 = 5$

○ $11 - 5 = 6$

○ $11 + 5 = 16$

○ $11 + 6 = 17$

GO ON ➡

21. Which shows a related addition fact?

$$13 - 6 = 7$$

○ $6 + 7 = 13$

○ $7 + 13 = 20$

○ $7 - 6 = 1$

○ $13 + 6 = 19$

22. Julian had 14 grapes. He gave 5 grapes to Lindsay. How many grapes does Julian have now?

○ 19

○ 11

○ 10

○ 9

23. Leah has 8 green apples and 4 red apples. How many apples does Leah have?

○ 4

○ 8

○ 12

○ 14

24. Mae has 2 rows of stickers. There are 4 stickers in each row. How many stickers does Mae have?

○ 2

○ 4

○ 6

○ 8

GO ON ➡

25. Tricia has 12 pencils to share equally with her classmate. Draw a picture to show how Tricia can share her pencils. How many pencils will Tricia keep?

Show your work.

Answer _____ pencils

---

26. Sarah uses 4 markers to color her picture. She has 11 markers in all. How many markers does Sarah **not** use?

Show your work.

Answer _____ markers

27. Write the differences. What is the next fact in each pattern?

$11 - 3 =$ ___ $10 - 3 =$ ___

$11 - 4 =$ ___ $11 - 3 =$ ___

$11 - 5 =$ ___ $12 - 3 =$ ___

Answer _____

---

28. There are 3 oranges in a bag. Mr. Johnson puts **4 more** oranges in the bag.

PART A

How many oranges are in the bag now?

Answer _____ oranges

PART B

Mr. Johnson puts **3 more** oranges in the bag. How many oranges are in the bag now?

Answer _____ oranges

Choose the correct answer.

1. Which shows a way to find the sum?

$$41 + 29$$

- ○ $41 + 30 = 71$
- ○ $40 + 20 = 60$
- ○ $40 + 30 = 70$
- ○ $50 + 30 = 80$

2. Which shows a way to find the sum?

$$66 + 16$$

- ○ $60 + 16 = 76$
- ○ $70 + 16 = 86$
- ○ $60 + 12 = 72$
- ○ $70 + 12 = 82$

3. What is the sum?

$$\begin{array}{r} 58 \\ 24 \\ +\ 3 \\ \hline \end{array}$$

- ○ 95
- ○ 85
- ○ 82
- ○ 27

4. What is the sum?

$$\begin{array}{r} 54 \\ 31 \\ +\ 17 \\ \hline \end{array}$$

- ○ 102
- ○ 85
- ○ 71
- ○ 48

GO ON

5. Jake has 57 stamps. He buys 37 more stamps. How many stamps does Jake have now?

○ 94

○ 87

○ 80

○ 20

6. There are 45 red grapes in a bowl. There are 18 green grapes in the bowl. How many grapes are in the bowl?

○ 37

○ 53

○ 63

○ 68

7. Lisa has 17 markers in her desk. She puts 29 more markers in the desk. How many markers are in the desk now?

○ 12

○ 32

○ 36

○ 46

8. There are 33 papers on a table. Ms. Smith puts 25 more papers on the table. How many papers are on the table now?

○ 12

○ 18

○ 58

○ 68

GO ON

9. Jenna counts 35 birds on a roof. She counts 26 birds on the ground. How many birds does Jenna see?

○ 51

○ 61

○ 65

○ 70

10. What is the sum?

$$\begin{array}{r} 23 \\ + 18 \\ \hline \end{array}$$

○ 41

○ 40

○ 31

○ 30

11. What is the sum?

$$\begin{array}{r} 58 \\ 17 \\ 23 \\ + 31 \\ \hline \end{array}$$

○ 98

○ 119

○ 125

○ 129

12. On four days this week, Caroline practiced her flute for 41 minutes, 38 minutes, 33 minutes, and 14 minutes. What is the number of minutes that Caroline practiced her flute?

○ 98

○ 107

○ 113

○ 126

GO ON

13. Gina and Eric play a game. Gina scores 26 points. Eric scores 31 points. How many points do Gina and Eric score?

○ 77

○ 67

○ 57

○ 55

14. What is the sum?

$$56 \\ + \ 67$$

○ 93

○ 107

○ 113

○ 123

15. What is the sum?

$$25 + 18 = \boxed{}$$

○ 33

○ 43

○ 53

○ 268

16. The table shows the number of books four children read this summer. How many books did Dora and Jason read?

Books Read This Summer	
Child	**Number of Books**
Dora	31
Kyle	38
Mark	29
Jason	27

○ 321   ○ 58

○ 69   ○ 50

GO ON

17. Savannah sees 18 butterflies at the park. Then she sees **8 more**. How can you find how many butterflies Savannah sees?

- ○ $18 - 8$
- ○ $18 + 6$
- ○ $18 - 5 - 2$
- ○ $18 + 2 + 6$

18. Break apart ones to make a ten. What is the sum?

$$89 + 5$$

- ○ 104
- ○ 94
- ○ 92
- ○ 84

19. James and Flora have 38 markers in all. Flora has 16 markers. How many markers does James have?

- ○ 22
- ○ 44
- ○ 54
- ○ 62

20. Alex has 46 beads. Chris has 33 beads. How many beads do they have?

- ○ 59
- ○ 63
- ○ 76
- ○ 79

GO ON

21. What is the sum?

$$\begin{array}{r} 16 \\ + 18 \\ \hline \end{array}$$

- ○ 23
- ○ 24
- ○ 33
- ○ 34

22. What is the sum?

$$\begin{array}{r} 59 \\ + 27 \\ \hline \end{array}$$

- ○ 86
- ○ 85
- ○ 76
- ○ 75

23. Jonas bought 13 blue marbles. He bought 38 purple marbles. How many marbles did Jonas buy?

- ○ 41
- ○ 45
- ○ 49
- ○ 51

24. Mark reads 13 pages of a book on Thursday. He reads 47 on Friday. How many pages does he read?

- ○ 34
- ○ 50
- ○ 60
- ○ 65

GO ON

25. There are 14 girls in a class. There are 8 boys. How many children are in the class? Draw quick pictures to solve.

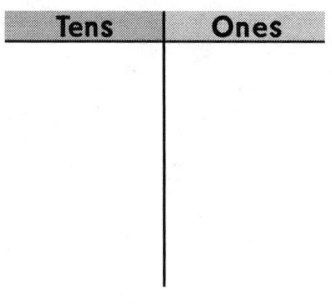

Tens	Ones

Answer _____ children

---

26. Greg says that he can find the sum of 40 + 53 without rewriting it. Explain how you can solve this problem using mental math.

_____

_____

GO ON

27. Mia buys 79 marbles. Which two bags does she buy?

Show your work.

Answer The bags with _____ marbles

---

28. Renee spends 22 minutes doing science homework. She spends 14 minutes doing history homework. She spends 33 minutes doing math homework.

PART A

How many minutes did Renee spend doing homework?

Answer _____ minutes

PART B

Renee spends another 32 minutes doing English homework. How many minutes did Renee spend doing homework now?

Answer _____ minutes

Name _____

Choose the correct answer.

1. There are 52 berries in a basket. Jan takes 16 berries out of the basket. How many berries are in the basket now?

○ 69

○ 44

○ 36

○ 34

2. Which shows a different way to write the subtraction problem?

$$48 - 23$$

○ $\begin{array}{r} 40 \\ - 20 \\ \hline 20 \end{array}$ ○ $\begin{array}{r} 18 \\ - 3 \\ \hline 15 \end{array}$

○ $\begin{array}{r} 48 \\ - 23 \\ \hline 25 \end{array}$ ○ $\begin{array}{r} 25 \\ - 23 \\ \hline 2 \end{array}$

3. Break apart the number you are subtracting. What is the difference?

$$44 - \underline{9} = \underline{\hspace{1cm}}$$

35   40   45   53
○   ○   ○   ○

4. Use the number line. Count up to find the difference.

$$53 - 46 = \underline{\hspace{1cm}}$$

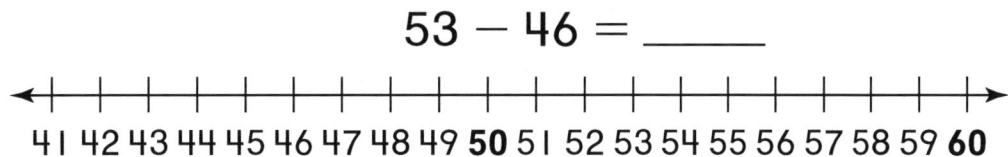

41 42 43 44 45 46 47 48 49 **50** 51 52 53 54 55 56 57 58 59 **60**

What is the difference?

6   7   8   9
○   ○   ○   ○

GO ON ➡

5. What is the difference?

$$6\ 2$$
$$-\ 2\ 5$$
_____

○ 87   ○ 43

○ 47   ○ 37

6. In which problem do you need to regroup to subtract?

○ 57 − 26

○ 39 − 18

○ 30 − 19

○ 73 − 63

7. Regroup if you need to. What is the difference?

Tens	Ones
☐	☐
4	6
− 1	9

○ 23   ○ 33

○ 27   ○ 37

8. Break apart the number you are subtracting. What is the difference?

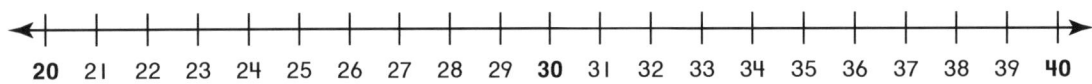

20 21 22 23 24 25 26 27 28 29 30 31 32 33 34 35 36 37 38 39 40

$$38 - 16 = \_\_\_\_$$

32   22   12   2
○   ○   ○   ○

GO ON

9. Mrs. Dobbs has 47 stickers. She gives away 12 stickers. How many stickers does she have left?

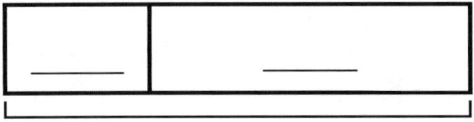

_____

○ 59

○ 35

○ 18

○ 5

10. Hannah makes 21 bracelets for the fair. Ladonne makes 5 more bracelets than Hannah. How many bracelets do they make in all?

○ 16

○ 26

○ 47

○ 52

11. Abby has 25 stamps. She buys 16 more stamps. Then she gives 12 stamps to Jeff. How many stamps does Abby have now?

○ 53

○ 41

○ 29

○ 13

12. There were 53 books on the shelf. Some of the books were checked out. Now there are 25 books on the shelf. Which number sentence can be used to find how many books were checked out?

○ $53 - \blacksquare = 25$

○ $53 + 25 = \blacksquare$

○ $28 + 53 = \blacksquare$

○ $28 - \blacksquare = 25$

GO ON ➡

Name _____

13. Subtract 14 from 43. Which shows the difference?

Tens	Ones

○ 2 tens 9 ones

○ 3 tens 1 one

○ 5 tens 7 ones

○ 8 tens 7 ones

14. Jason has 52 baseball cards. Kim has 28 baseball cards. How many more baseball cards does Jason have than Kim?

○ 36

○ 34

○ 24

○ 6

15. Break apart ones to subtract. What is the difference?

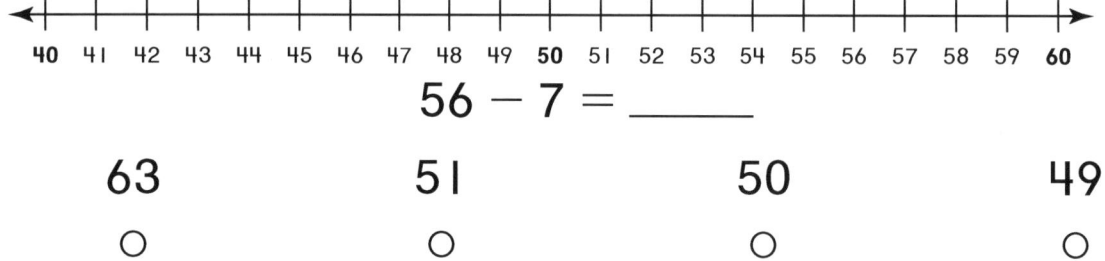

$$56 - 7 = \underline{\hspace{1cm}}$$

63   51   50   49
○   ○   ○   ○

16. Use the number line. Count up to find the difference.

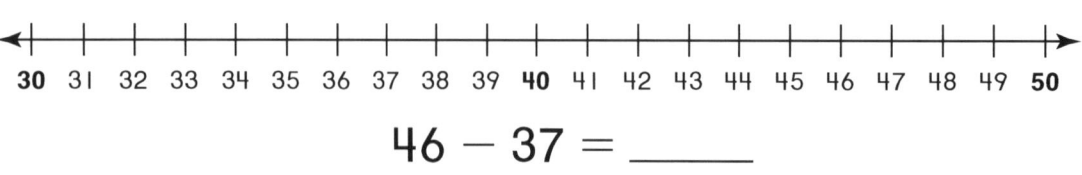

$$46 - 37 = \underline{\hspace{1cm}}$$

1   9   11   19
○   ○   ○   ○

GO ON

17. What is the difference?

```
    5 0
  - 2 6
  ─────
```

○ 24

○ 25

○ 36

○ 76

18. What is the difference?

```
    3 5
  - 1 4
  ─────
```

○ 49

○ 21

○ 29

○ 11

19. What is the difference?

Tens	Ones
☐	☐
6	2
− 2	9

○ 91

○ 81

○ 47

○ 33

20. Draw a quick picture to solve. What is the difference?

Tens	Ones
☐	☐
4	2
− 1	7

Tens	Ones

○ 25

○ 35

○ 39

○ 59

GO ON

21. Break apart the number you are subtracting. What is the difference?

$$51 - 17 = \underline{\qquad}$$

34	44	46	68
○	○	○	○

---

22. Juan has 16 candles. Melanie has **3 more** candles than Juan. How many candles do they have altogether?

○ 13   ○ 32

○ 19   ○ 35

23. Rosa has some stickers. She gives away 35 stickers. Now Rosa has 19 stickers. Which number sentence can be used to find how many stickers Rosa had to start?

○ $35 - \blacksquare = 19$

○ $\blacksquare - 35 = 19$

○ $\blacksquare + 19 = 35$

○ $54 + \blacksquare = 73$

---

24. A store sells 34 shirts. 7 shirts are blue. The rest of the shirts are white. How many white shirts does the store sell?

17	21	27	41
○	○	○	○

GO ON

25. Kent's book has 64 pages. Kent reads 27 pages in the morning. He reads **18 more** pages that night. How many pages does Kent need to read to finish the book? Complete the bar models for the steps you do to solve the problem.

Answer _____ more pages

---

26. Subtract 18 from 35. What is the difference?

Show your work.

Answer _____

27. What is 81 – 16?

Show your work.

Answer _____

GO ON

Name _____

28. Dan has 29 animal pictures. Kayla has 37 animal pictures.

PART A

Who has **more** animal pictures? How many **more**? Use a bar model to solve.

Show your work.

Answer _____ has _____ more animal pictures.

PART B

Dan gets **I I more** animal pictures. Who has **more** animal pictures now? How many **more**? Use a bar model to solve.

Show your work.

Answer _____ has _____ more animal pictures.

Name _____

Choose the correct answer.

1. What is the difference?

Hundreds	Tens	Ones
	☐	☐
3	8	2
− 1	5	4

○ 128   ○ 228

○ 232   ○ 238

2. Meg had 432 stickers. She gave 216 of the stickers to a classmate. How many stickers does Meg have left?

○ 248

○ 226

○ 224

○ 216

3. What is the difference?

Hundreds	Tens	Ones
☐	☐	☐
3	1	7
− 1	2	5

○ 182

○ 192

○ 292

○ 432

4. What is the sum?

Hundreds	Tens	Ones
☐	☐	
4	7	1
+ 2	3	4

○ 245

○ 605

○ 705

○ 715

GO ON ▶

5. Add 213 and 151. What is the sum?

Hundreds	Tens	Ones
□ □	∣	o o o
□	∣∣∣∣∣	o

○ 364   ○ 314   ○ 264   ○ 263

---

6. A bird watcher counted 163 white birds and 185 black birds. How many birds did she count?

$$163 \longrightarrow 100 + 60 + 3$$
$$+\ 185 \longrightarrow +\ 100 + 80 + 5$$

○ 248   ○ 258   ○ 348   ○ 358

---

7. Sydney's class collected 368 cans for recycling. Ramon's class collected 413 cans. How many cans did the two classes collect in all?

○ 771   ○ 871

○ 781   ○ 881

8. What is the sum?

Hundreds	Tens	Ones
	□	
5	2	7
+ 1	4	8

○ 575   ○ 675

○ 665   ○ 765

GO ON

9. What is the sum?

```
    2 9 9
+   2 3 7
```

- ○ 426
- ○ 436
- ○ 526
- ○ 536

10. At the store, there are 863 rocks and shells. There are 121 rocks. How many shells are there?

- ○ 642
- ○ 742
- ○ 842
- ○ 984

11. What is the difference?

```
    4 6 2
-   1 9 5
```

- ○ 267
- ○ 333
- ○ 367
- ○ 377

12. What is the difference?

```
    5 0 6
-   3 2 9
```

- ○ 223
- ○ 187
- ○ 183
- ○ 177

GO ON

13. What is the difference?

Hundreds	Tens	Ones
	☐	☐
4	5	2
− 2	3	7

○ 225   ○ 125

○ 215   ○ 115

14. What is the sum?

Hundreds	Tens	Ones
	☐	☐
5	8	2
+ 2	3	7

○ 719   ○ 819

○ 755   ○ 829

15. What is the sum?

Hundreds	Tens	Ones
	☐	☐
6	7	4
+ 1	8	1

○ 855

○ 765

○ 755

○ 493

16. What is the sum?

Hundreds	Tens	Ones
	☐	
3	2	8
+ 5	1	4

○ 832

○ 834

○ 842

○ 942

GO ON

17. Add 254 and 215. What is the sum?

Hundreds	Tens	Ones
☐ ☐	‖‖‖	○○○○
☐ ☐			○○○○○

○ 454　　　　○ 459　　　　○ 464　　　　○ 469

---

18. Which shows 524 broken apart into hundreds, tens, and ones?

○ 500 + 20 + 40

○ 500 + 20 + 4

○ 50 + 20 + 4

○ 50 + 2 + 4

---

19. What is the sum?

```
    1 5 8
 +  1 6 2
```

○ 210　　　○ 320

○ 220　　　○ 330

20. What is the sum?

```
    2 3 8
 +  2 2 5
```

○ 563　　　○ 453

○ 463　　　○ 413

21. There are 417 children at the festival. 288 of the children are girls. Which problem shows how many of the children are boys?

- ○   3   9   5
     − 2   1   8

- ○   4   8   0
     − 3   4   1

- ○   4   1   7
     − 2   8   8

- ○   3   6   0
     − 3   2   4

22. There are 594 children at the museum. There are 235 boys. How many girls are at the museum?

- ○ 829
- ○ 369
- ○ 361
- ○ 359

23. A farmer has 305 sheep. She moves 263 sheep into a field. Which sentence describes a step in finding how many sheep are left?

- ○ Regroup 1 ten as 10 ones.
- ○ Subtract 0 tens from 6 tens.
- ○ Regroup 1 hundred as 10 tens.
- ○ Subtract 2 hundreds from 3 hundreds.

24. What is the difference?

    7   0   1
− 5   4   6

- ○ 145
- ○ 155
- ○ 245
- ○ 265

GO ON

Name _____

25. Louis wants to add 231 and 248. Help Louis solve this problem. Draw quick pictures. Write how many hundreds, tens, and ones in all. Write the number.

Hundreds	Tens	Ones

_____ hundreds _____ tens _____ ones

Answer _____

---

26. Mr. Ramos picks 327 apples. He gives 169 apples away. How many apples does Mr. Ramos still have?

Show your work.

Answer _____ apples

27. A store sells 104 DVDs and 88 CDs. Describe how you would find how many **more** DVDs the store sells than CDs.

_____
_____
_____

28. Riley used this method to find the sum of $538 + 254$.

$$
\begin{array}{r}
538 \\
+\ 254 \\
\hline
700 \\
80 \\
+\ 12 \\
\hline
792
\end{array}
$$

PART A

Describe how Riley solves addition problems.

_____
_____

PART B

Use Riley's method to find the following sum.

$$
\begin{array}{r}
364 \\
+\ 217 \\
\hline
\end{array}
$$

Answer _____

Name _____

Choose the correct answer.

1. What is the time on the clock?

- ○ 6:00
- ○ 8:00
- ○ 8:30
- ○ 9:30

2. What is the time on the clock?

- ○ 9:00
- ○ 9:30
- ○ 12:00
- ○ 12:30

3. What is the time on the clock?

- ○ 7:40
- ○ 7:50
- ○ 8:00
- ○ 8:50

4. What is the time on the clock?

- ○ 1:03
- ○ 1:15
- ○ 3:05
- ○ 3:10

GO ON

5. What is the total value of this money?

○ $1.15   ○ $1.30

○ $1.26   ○ $1.35

6. Kim has 60 cents. Which set of coins shows this amount?

○     ○

○      ○

7. Which combination of coins has a value of 75 cents?

○ 2 quarters

○ 10 nickels and 5 dimes

○ 1 quarter, 2 dimes, and 3 nickels

○ 6 dimes, 2 nickels, and 5 pennies

8. Count on. What is the total value of these coins?

○ 37¢   ○ 28¢

○ 32¢   ○ 17¢

GO ON ➡

9. Which clock shows quarter past 8?

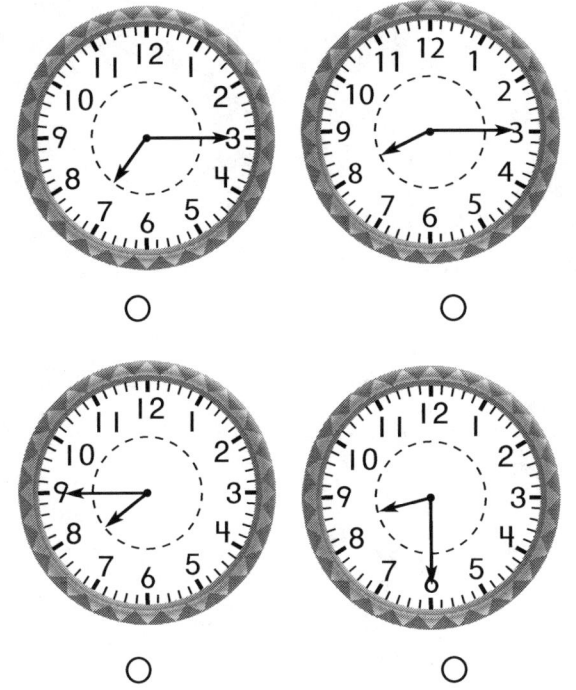

○   ○

○   ○

10. Kareem has these coins in his wallet.

What is the total value of these coins?

○ 31¢   ○ 51¢

○ 36¢   ○ 77¢

---

11. Jessie buys a book that costs $1.00. Which coins does she use to buy the book?

○   5 pennies

○   5 dimes

○ 10 nickels

○ 10 dimes

12. One night, Mrs. Rivera saw a rocket launch at the time shown on the clock.

At what time did Mrs. Rivera see the rocket launch?

○ 12:40 A.M.   ○ 12:40 P.M.

○ 8:00 A.M.   ○ 8:00 P.M.

13. Petra's soccer practice starts at 4:00.
Which clock shows 4:00?

○   ○   ○   ○

14. Lee goes to bed at 8:30. Which clock shows 8:30?

○   ○   ○   ○

15. Sasha eats breakfast at the time shown on the clock.

At what time does Sasha eat breakfast?

○ 7:08   ○ 8:08

○ 7:40   ○ 8:40

16. Count on. What is the total value of these coins?

○   7¢

○   11¢

○   25¢

○   45¢

GO ON

17. Fred has these coins in his pocket.

How much money does Fred have in his pocket?

○ 75¢   ○ 25¢

○ 55¢   ○ 15¢

18. Count on. What is the total value of these coins?

○ 28¢

○ 25¢

○ 13¢

○ 8¢

---

19. Which clock shows 20 minutes past 3?

○   ○   ○   ○

---

20. What is the total value of these coins?

33¢   42¢   51¢   60¢

○   ○   ○   ○

GO ON ➤

21. Which group of coins has a total value of $1.00?

22. James paid for a drink with this money. How much did James pay?

○ $1.41   ○ $1.46   ○ $1.56   ○ $1.61

23. Marta pays $1.80 for a snack. What is one way to show $1.80?

○ one $1 bill, 2 quarters, and 3 nickels
○ one $1 bill, 3 quarters, and 1 dime
○ 5 quarters, 2 dimes, and 1 nickel
○ 7 quarters and 1 nickel

24. The clock shows the time that Kyle got on the school bus this morning. At what time did he get on the bus?

○ 7:30 P.M.   ○ 7:30 A.M.

○ 9:35 P.M.   ○ 9:35 A.M.

25. Antoine gave Fran these coins. Antoine says he gave Fran $1.00. Is Antoine correct? Explain.

Answer _____

_____

26. The clock shows the time Sarah starts getting ready for bed. Write the time, and tell how you knew whether it is A.M. or P.M.

Answer _____

_____

GO ON

27. Alfredo buys a baseball card for 65¢. Draw and label coins to show a total value of 65¢.

Answer

---

28. Hannah gave her sister these coins.

PART A

Write the value of the coins, and explain how you found the total value.

Answer _____

PART B

Draw more coins so the total is 96¢.

Answer

Choose the correct answer.

Use the line plot for Exercises 1–2.

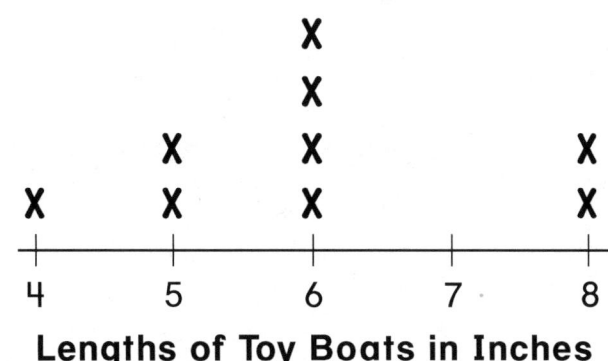

Lengths of Toy Boats in Inches

1. Suppose one of the toy boats that is 5 inches long breaks and is thrown away. How many 5-inch boats should the line plot now show?

   ○ 0   ○ 1   ○ 2   ○ 3

2. How many toy boats are 4 inches long?

   ○ 1   ○ 2   ○ 4   ○ 6

3. Mia measures the length of a book to the nearest inch. It is about 12 inches long. Which is the same as 12 inches?

   ○   1 foot

   ○   2 feet

   ○   6 feet

   ○ 12 feet

4. Which sentence is **most** likely to be **true**?

   ○ The boy is 40 feet tall.

   ○ The building is 30 feet tall.

   ○ The street is 12 inches wide.

   ○ The driveway is 35 inches long.

5. Each tile is about 1 inch long. Which is the best choice for the length of the ribbon?

○ about 1 inch

○ about 2 inches

○ about 4 inches

○ about 5 inches

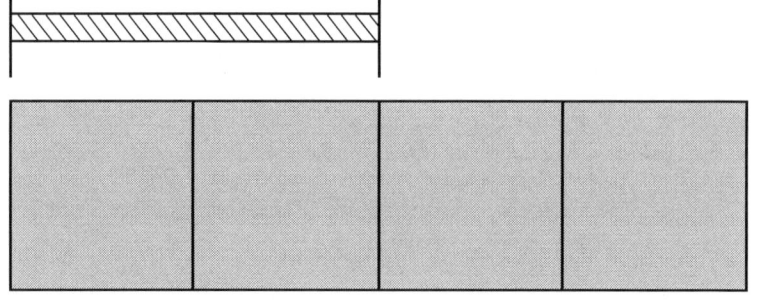

---

6. Owen made a paper clip chain that was 18 inches long. Then he removed 9 inches of paper clips from the chain. How long is the paper clip chain now?

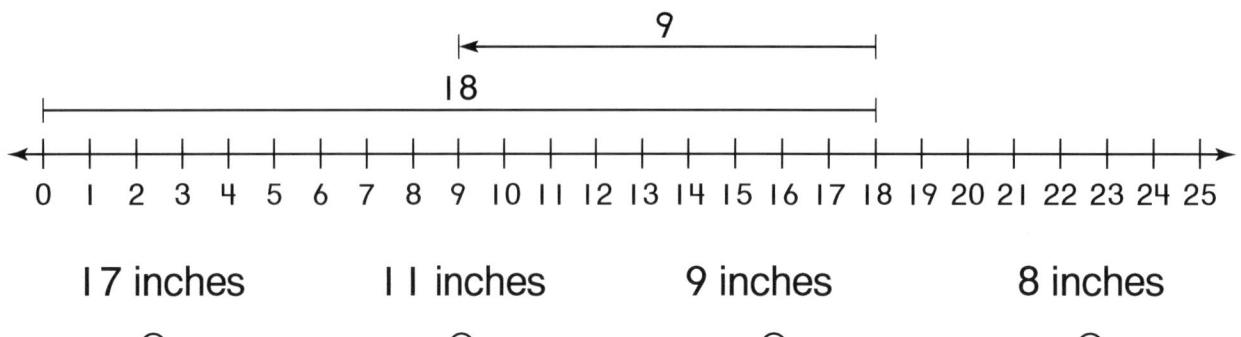

17 inches   11 inches   9 inches   8 inches

○   ○   ○   ○

---

7. The bead is 1 inch long. What is the best estimate for the length of the string?

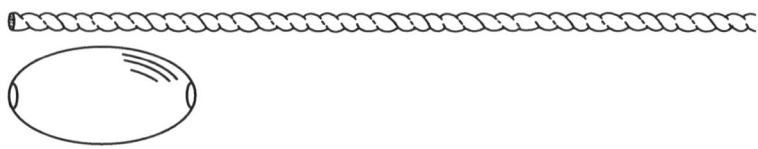

10 inches   7 inches   4 inches   1 inch

○   ○   ○   ○

8. Use an inch ruler. What is the length of the lip balm to the nearest inch?

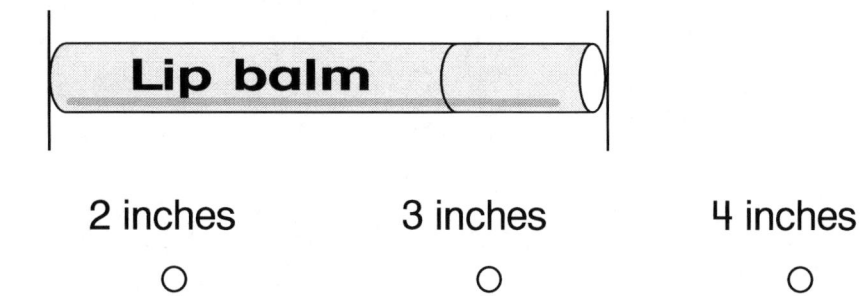

1 inch	2 inches	3 inches	4 inches
○	○	○	○

9. Use an inch ruler. What is the length of the string to the nearest inch?

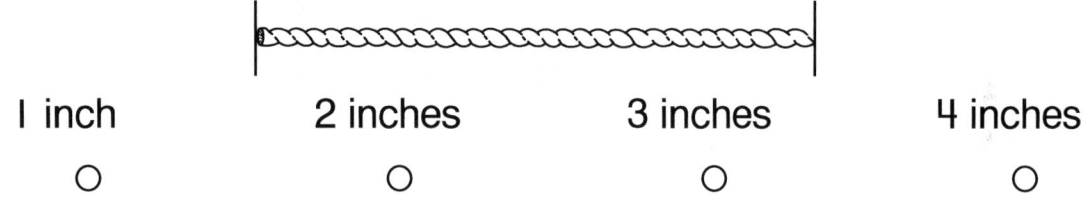

1 inch	2 inches	3 inches	4 inches
○	○	○	○

10. Which is the **best** estimate for the width of a real classroom door using 1-foot tiles?

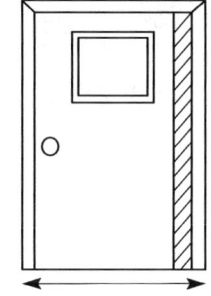

○ 1 tile

○ 3 tiles

○ 8 tiles

○ 20 tiles

11. Use your ruler.

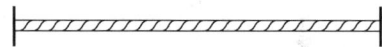

Which is the best choice for the length of the yarn?

○ about 2 inches

○ about 3 inches

○ about 4 inches

○ about 5 inches

GO ON →

Name _____

Use the line plot for Questions 12–13.

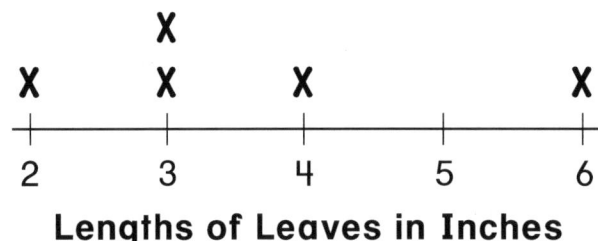

Lengths of Leaves in Inches

12. How many leaves does the line plot show?

  ○ 1   ○ 5

  ○ 2   ○ 8

13. How many leaves are 5 inches long?

  ○ 0   ○ 2

  ○ 1   ○ 4

14. Leah shows her friend how to use a ruler to measure length. Which sentence is true?

  ○ 1 foot is a shorter length than 1 inch.

  ○ 1 inch is a shorter length than 1 foot.

  ○ 1 inch is the same length as 1 foot.

  ○ Inches are not used to measure length.

15. Sam wants to measure the distance around a can of soup. Which is the best tool for Sam to use?

  ○ cup

  ○ measuring tape

  ○ large paper clip

  ○ pencil

GO ON →

16. Each tile is about 1 inch long. Which is the
best choice for the length of the straw?

○ about 1 inch

○ about 3 inches

○ about 4 inches

○ about 5 inches

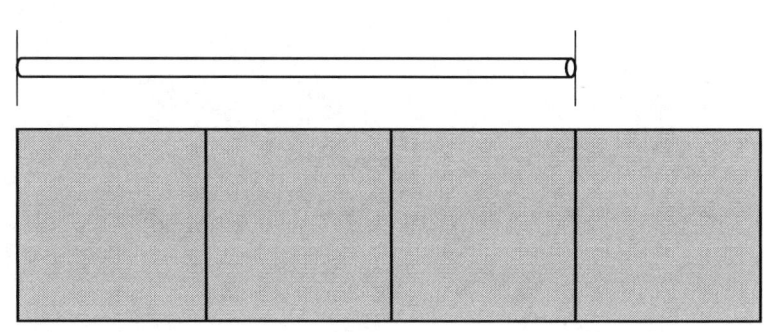

---

17. Lin has a string that is 6 inches long and a string
that is 11 inches long. How many inches of string
does Lin have altogether?

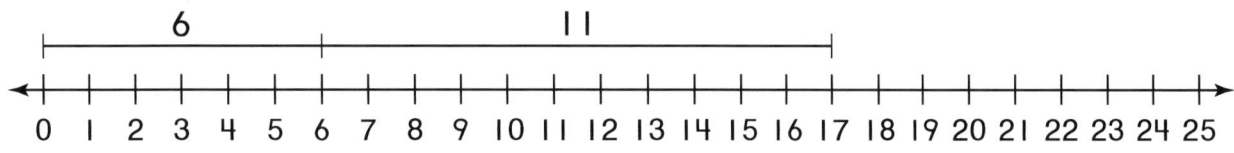

19 inches	17 inches	11 inches	5 inches
○	○	○	○

---

18. The bead is 1 inch long. What is the best
estimate for the length of the string?

7 inches	5 inches	3 inches	1 inch
○	○	○	○

GO ON

19. Use an inch ruler. What is the length of the crayon to the nearest inch?

- ○ 2 inches
- ○ 3 inches
- ○ 4 inches
- ○ 5 inches

20. Suppose 1-inch tiles are used to estimate the length of a football. Which sentence is correct?

- ○ The football is less than 2 tiles long.
- ○ The football is about 6 tiles long.
- ○ The football is about 12 tiles long.
- ○ The football is more than 50 tiles long.

21. Use your ruler to measure the string.

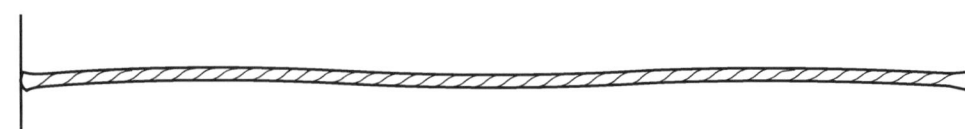

What is the best choice for the length of the string?

- ○ about 3 inches
- ○ about 4 inches
- ○ about 5 inches
- ○ about 6 inches

22. Use your ruler to measure the marker.

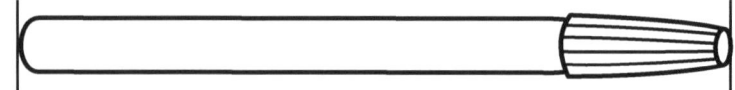

What is the best choice for the length of the marker?

- ○ about 5 inches
- ○ about 4 inches
- ○ about 3 inches
- ○ about 2 inches

23. Owen wants to measure the length of a chalkboard. Should he use tiles, an inch ruler, or a yardstick? Explain your choice of tool.

Answer _____

_____

---

24. Meg has a ribbon that is 9 inches long. She has another ribbon that is 11 inches long. How many inches of ribbon does Meg have? Draw a diagram to solve.

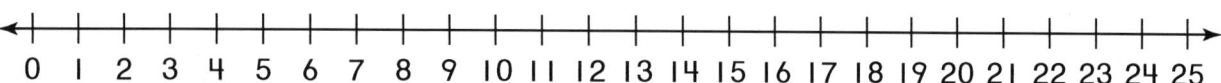

0 1 2 3 4 5 6 7 8 9 10 11 12 13 14 15 16 17 18 19 20 21 22 23 24 25

Show your work.

Answer Meg has _____ inches of ribbon.

GO ON

25. Zach uses tiles to measure a straw. Each tile is 1 inch long. Zach says the straw is 4 inches long. Is he correct? Explain.

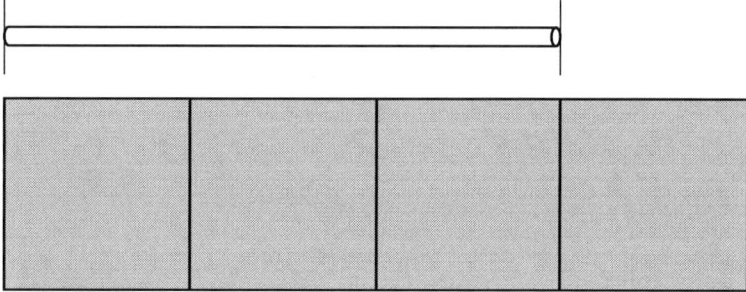

Answer _____

_____

---

26. Marta measured some crayons in a box.

Lengths of Crayons	
5 inches	4 inches
2 inches	4 inches
3 inches	

PART A

Use the data in the list to make a line plot.

Answer

PART B

Suppose the crayon that is 5 inches long broke. Now it is 3 inches long. Explain how the line plot should be changed.

Answer _____

_____

_____

Choose the correct answer.

1. Which words make the sentence true?

I centimeter is _____ I meter.

○ longer than

○ shorter than

○ the same as

---

2. Mandy used unit cubes to measure the length of a straw. Which is the best choice for the length of the straw?

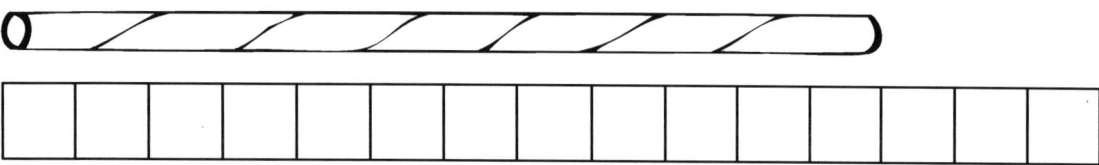

○ 12 centimeters   ○ 14 centimeters

○ 13 centimeters   ○ 15 centimeters

---

3. Ken used unit cubes to measure the length of a stick. Which is the best choice for the length of the stick?

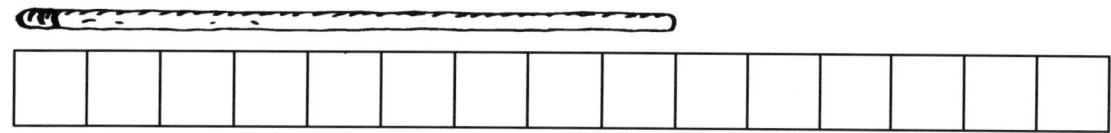

○ 6 centimeters   ○ 9 centimeters

○ 7 centimeters   ○ 16 centimeters   **GO ON** ➡

4. Estimate the length of a real horse. Which is the **best** answer?

○ The horse is about 3 meters long.

○ The horse is less than 1 meter long.

○ The horse is about 6 centimeters long.

○ The horse is less than 10 centimeters long.

5. Ms. Diaz had a board that was 22 centimeters long. Then she cut 8 centimeters off the board. How long is the board now?

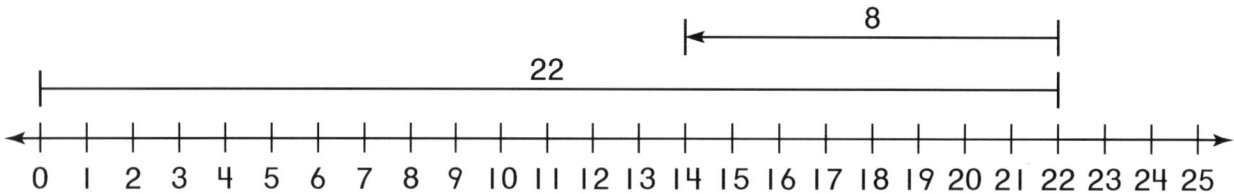

○ 30 centimeters   ○ 14 centimeters

○ 22 centimeters   ○ 8 centimeters

6. Which number sentence can be used to find how much longer the ribbon is than the paper clip?

 9 centimeters

 5 centimeters

○ 9 + 5 = 14   ○ 9 − 5 = 4

○ 9 + 4 = 13   ○ 5 − 4 = 1

GO ON

7. The string is about 2 centimeters long.

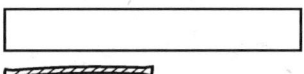

Which is the **best** estimate for
the length of the strip of paper?

○ 1 centimeter   ○ 4 centimeters

○ 2 centimeters   ○ 6 centimeters

8. The crayon is about 8 centimeters long.

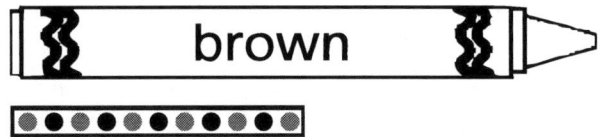

Which is the **best** estimate for
the length of the ribbon?

○ 8 centimeters   ○ 4 centimeters

○ 6 centimeters   ○ 2 centimeters

9. Use a centimeter ruler. What is the length
of the yarn to the nearest centimeter?

○ 2 centimeters   ○ 4 centimeters

○ 3 centimeters   ○ 5 centimeters

10. Which sentence makes the **most** sense?

○ A car is 6 centimeters long.

○ A sidewalk is 2 meters wide.

○ A swimming pool is 50 centimeters long.

○ A computer keyboard is 42 meters wide.

11. Use a centimeter ruler. How much longer is the pencil than the string?

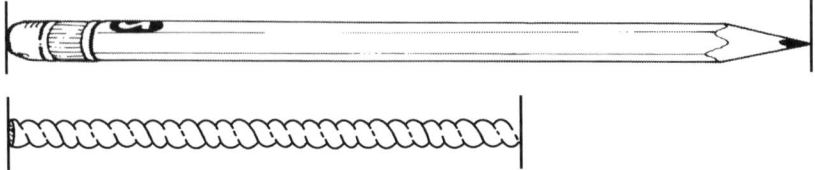

○ 18 centimeters longer   ○ 7 centimeters longer

○ 11 centimeters longer   ○ 4 centimeters longer

12. Susan uses unit cubes to measure the length of the yarn. What is the **best** estimate for the length of the yarn?

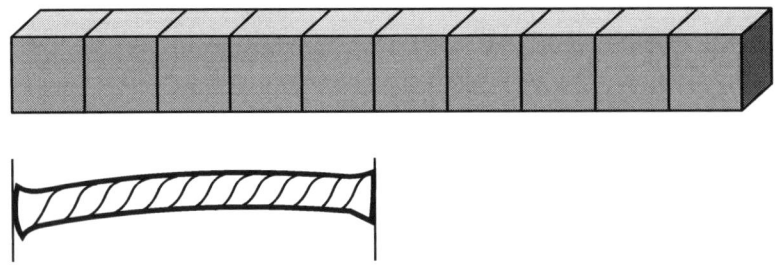

○ 2 centimeters   ○ 5 centimeters

○ 3 centimeters   ○ 9 centimeters

13. Which is the **best** estimate for the length of a window?

○ 10 meters   ○ 7 meters   ○ 5 meters   ○ 2 meters

14. Ann has a rope that is 12 centimeters long. Hiro has a rope that is 5 centimeters long. How many centimeters of rope do they have altogether?

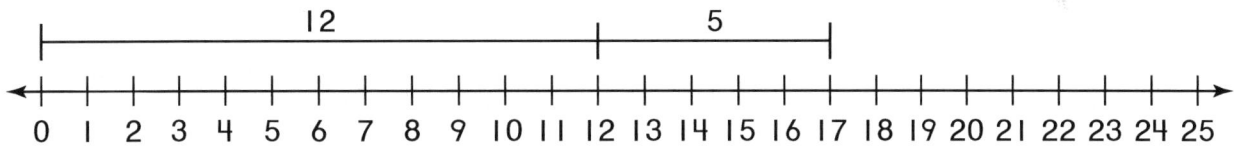

○ 17 centimeters   ○ 12 centimeters
○ 16 centimeters   ○ 7 centimeters

15. Roy drew a mark that was 15 centimeters long. Then he erased 6 centimeters from the mark. How long is the mark now?

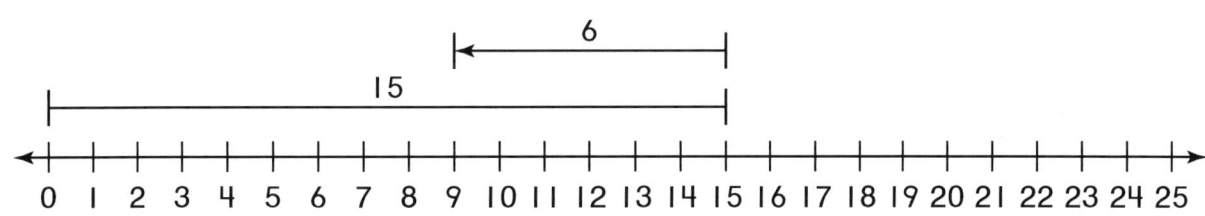

○ 21 centimeters   ○ 9 centimeters
○ 15 centimeters   ○ 6 centimeters

GO ON

Name _____

16. Measure the length of each object. Which describes the length of the crayon compared to the length of the yarn?

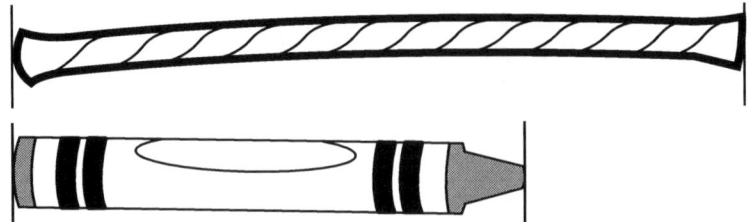

- ○ 3 centimeters shorter
- ○ 3 centimeters longer
- ○ 7 centimeters shorter
- ○ 7 centimeters longer

17. The ribbon is about 4 centimeters long.

Which is the **best** estimate for the length of the straw?

- ○ 3 centimeters
- ○ 7 centimeters
- ○ 4 centimeters
- ○ 9 centimeters

18. Measure the length of the rope to the nearest centimeter. What is the **best** estimate for the length of the rope?

- ○ 10 centimeters
- ○ 13 centimeters
- ○ 12 centimeters
- ○ 15 centimeters

19. Use a centimeter ruler. What is the length of the ribbon to the nearest centimeter?

- ○ 5 centimeters
- ○ 7 centimeters
- ○ 6 centimeters
- ○ 8 centimeters

20. The paintbrush is about 7 centimeters long. Gavin says the feather is about 8 centimeters long. Ray says the feather is about 5 centimeters long. Which boy has the **better** estimate? Explain.

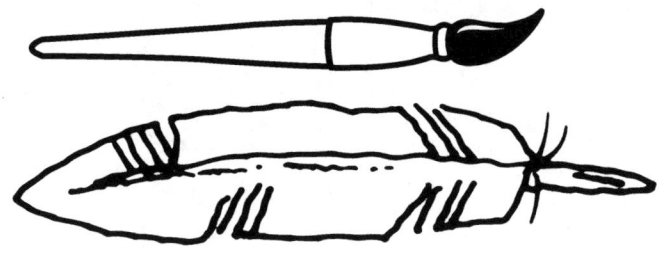

Answer _____

_____

21. Alberto uses 8 centimeters of wire for a science project. He uses another 15 centimeters of wire for another project. How many centimeters does he use? Draw a diagram to solve.

0 1 2 3 4 5 6 7 8 9 10 11 12 13 14 15 16 17 18 19 20 21 22 23 24 25

Answer _____ centimeters

22. Elizabeth has a piece of ribbon that is 25 centimeters long. She cuts off a piece of ribbon to use to wrap a gift. Elizabeth's ribbon is now 7 centimeters long. How many centimeters of ribbon did Elizabeth use to wrap the gift? Write a number sentence and solve.

Show your work.

Answer _____ centimeters

23. Alexis has these three pieces of string left over from wrapping up bundles of wood.

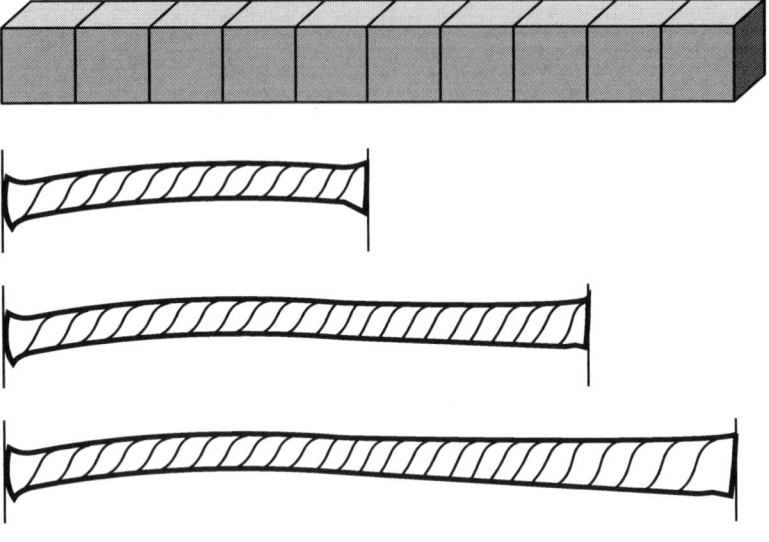

PART A

What are the lengths of each piece of string?

Answer _____

PART B

Which two pieces of string have a total length of 13 centimeters? Explain how you found this.

Answer _____

_____

_____

Choose the correct answer.

Use the bar graph for Questions 1–4.

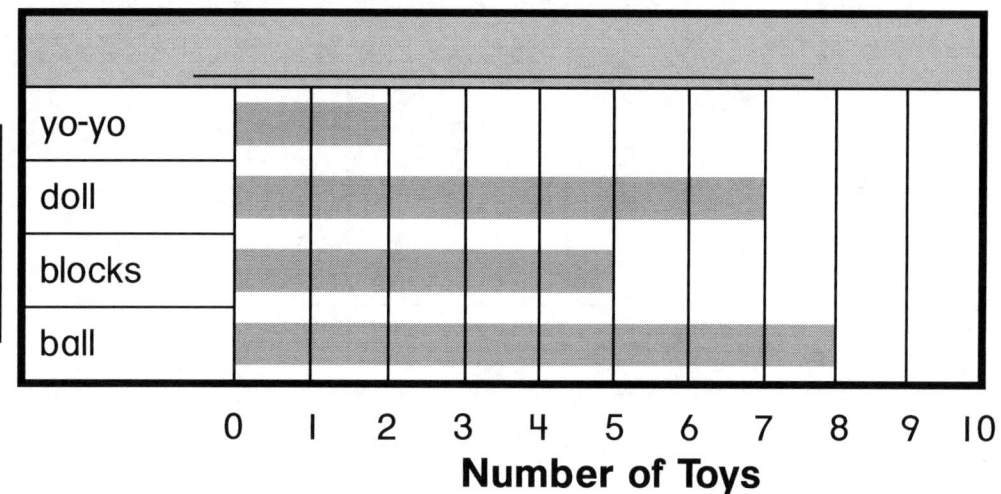

1. Which is the **best** label for the rows in the bar graph?

○ Toy   ○ Children

○ Yo-Yos   ○ Game

2. Which is the **best** title for the bar graph?

○ Books We Like   ○ Children's Dolls

○ Favorite Yo-Yo   ○ Toys in the Store

3. How many more dolls than blocks are in the store?

○ 1   ○ 5

○ 2   ○ 7

4. How many balls are in the store?

○ 5   ○ 8

○ 7   ○ 10

Use the picture graph for Questions 5–8.

Pets We Have				
dog	☆	☆	☆	
cat	☆			
fish	☆	☆	☆	☆
bird	☆	☆		

Key: Each ☆ stands for 1 child.

5. How many more children have fish than a dog?

○ 0   ○ 1   ○ 2   ○ 3

6. What are two animals that a total of 6 children have?

○ dog and cat   ○ bird and cat

○ fish and dog   ○ fish and bird

7. 2 more children have cats. Now how many ☆ should be in the cat row of the picture graph?

○ 3

○ 4

○ 5

○ 6

8. 3 children have a hamster. Which shows a hamster row for the picture graph?

○ ☆ ☆ ☆ ☆ ☆

○ ☆ ☆ ☆ ☆

○ ☆ ☆ ☆

○ ☆ ☆

GO ON ➡

Use the tally chart for Questions 9–12.

Favorite Month	
Month	**Tally**
May	卌
June	卌 I
July	IIII
August	III

9. Which statement is **true**?

○ More than 10 children like July or August.

○ June is the least favorite month.

○ More children like May than August.

○ Most children like July.

10. Which month did the **most** children choose?

○ May

○ June

○ July

○ August

11. Which month did the **fewest** children choose?

○ May   ○ July

○ June   ○ August

12. **7 more** children were asked their favorite month. 6 children like May the **most** and 1 child likes August the **most**. Now which month is chosen as favorite by the **most** children?

○ May   ○ July

○ June   ○ August

13. Joe read for 5 hours in Week 1, 3 hours in Week 2, and 2 hours in Week 3. Which bar graph shows this data?

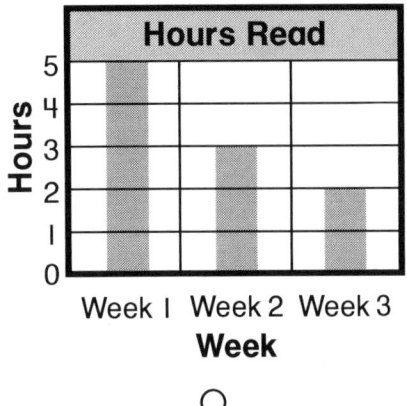

○

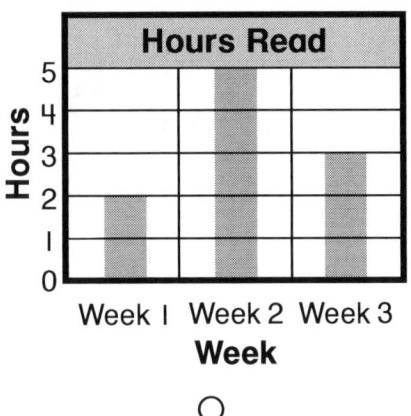

○

Use the bar graph for Questions 14–16.

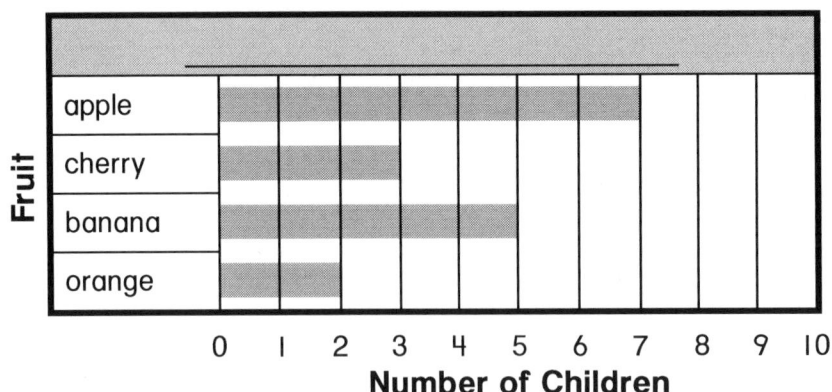

14. Which could be the title of the bar graph?

○ Our Pets   ○ Apples   ○ Favorite Fruit   ○ Books Read

15. How many **more** children chose banana or cherry than apple?

○ 1   ○ 2   ○ 3   ○ 4

16. Which of the following sentences is **true**?

○ 6 children chose banana.

○ 7 children chose cherry or orange.

○ Apple was the most popular.

○ 3 more children chose banana than cherry.

Use the picture graph for Questions 17–20.

Favorite Sports					
hockey	☺	☺			
football	☺	☺	☺		
soccer	☺	☺	☺	☺	☺
basketball	☺	☺	☺		

Key: Each ☺ stands for 1 child.

17. How many children chose soccer?

○ 2   ○ 4

○ 3   ○ 5

18. How many children in all chose football or hockey?

○ 8   ○ 3

○ 5   ○ 2

19. 1 more child chose basketball. Now how many ☺ should be in the basketball row of the picture graph?

○ 2

○ 4

○ 5

○ 6

20. 4 children like baseball the best. Which shows a baseball row for the picture graph?

○ ☺ ☺ ☺ ☺

○ ☺ ☺ ☺

○ ☺ ☺

○ ☺

GO ON ➡

Use the tally chart for Questions 21–24.

Favorite Animal	
Animal	**Tally**
lion	ⅢⅡ
bear	|||
monkey	||
giraffe	ⅢⅡ ||

21. Which statement is **true**?

   ○ 8 children chose
     giraffe.

   ○ 17 children voted
     in all.

   ○ 5 children voted for
     bear.

   ○ More children chose
     monkey than lion.

22. Which animal did the **fewest**
children choose?

   ○ lion

   ○ bear

   ○ monkey

   ○ giraffe

23. Which animal did the **most**
children choose?

   ○ lion   ○ monkey

   ○ bear   ○ giraffe

24. How many children chose
lion?

   ○ 3   ○ 5

   ○ 4   ○ 6

GO ON ➡

25. Use the tally chart to complete the picture graph.
How many children chose art?

Favorite School Subject	
math	IIII
reading	III
science	II
art	III

Favorite School Subject					
math					
reading					
science					
art					

Key: Each ☺ stands for I child.

Answer _____ children

---

26. Karina counted the number of sit-ups she did each day.
Describe how the number of sit-ups changed from
Monday to Thursday. Make a bar graph to solve the problem.

Monday – 3 sit-ups   Wednesday – 6 sit-ups

Tuesday – 5 sit-ups   Thursday – 8 sit-ups

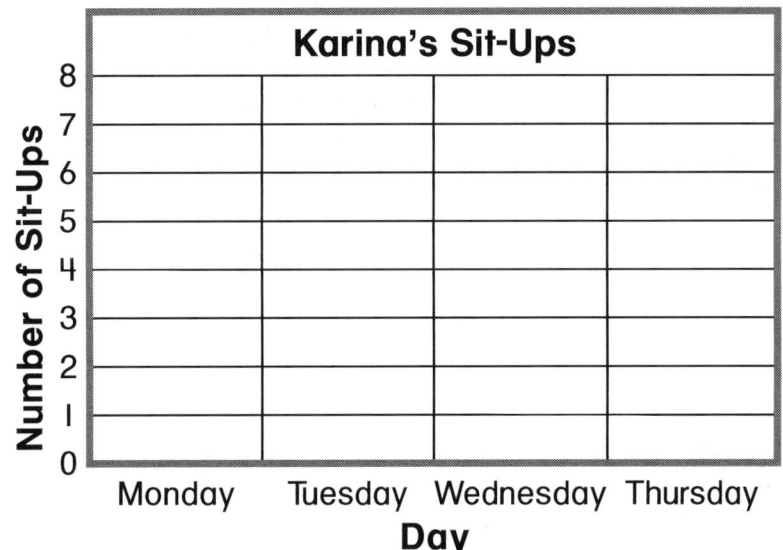

Answer _____
_____

GO ON

27. Eric asked some friends to name their favorite sandwich. Use the data to complete the bar graph. How many children name turkey?

4 children name ham.

6 children name turkey.

1 child names cheese.

3 children name jelly.

Answer _____ friends

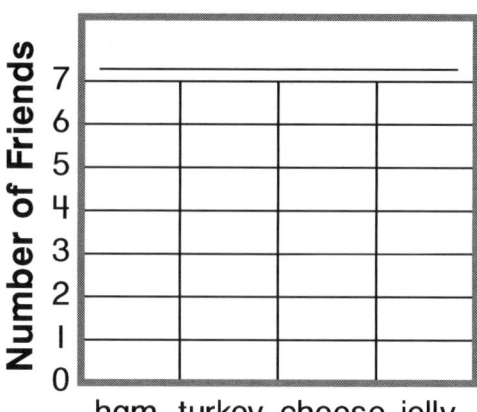

28. Nathan asked his friends to choose their favorite sport. He wrote the results in the picture graph below.

Favorite Sports					
hockey	☺	☺			
football	☺	☺	☺		
soccer	☺	☺	☺	☺	☺
basketball	☺	☺	☺		

Key: Each ☺ stands for 1 child.

PART A

Nathan asks **3 more** friends which sport they like **best.** 2 friends choose football and 1 friend chooses hockey. Which sport is the **most** chosen now? Explain.

Answer _____

_____

_____

PART B

How many children are there in all now?

Answer _____ children

Name _____

Choose the correct answer.

1. What is the shape of this sign?

○ triangle

○ quadrilateral

○ pentagon

○ hexagon

2. Alex built this rectangular prism. How many unit cubes did Alex use?

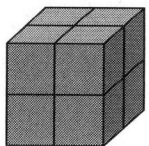

○ 7

○ 8

○ 16

○ 18

3. Which shape has **fewer** than 4 angles?

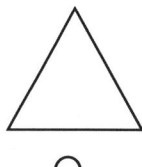 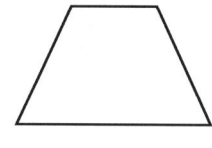

○   ○

 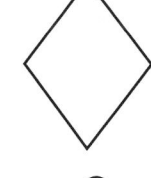

○   ○

4. Lisa used square tiles to cover this rectangle. How many square tiles did she use to cover the rectangle?

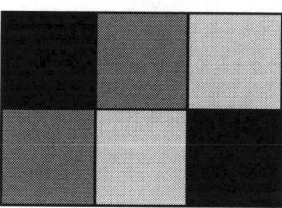

○ 4

○ 6

○ 8

○ 9

GO ON ➡

5. Paul makes a hexagon and a triangle with straws. He uses one straw for each side of a shape. How many straws does Paul need?

- ○ 8
- ○ 9
- ○ 10
- ○ 11

6. Which shape shows fourths?

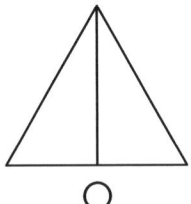
○

○

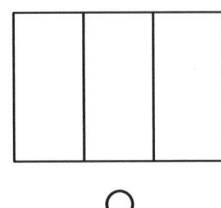
○

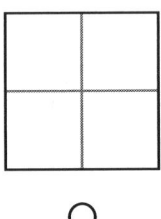
○

7. Which of these shapes is a cube?

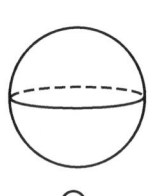
○

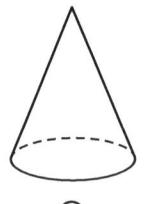
○

○

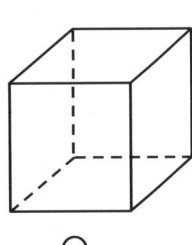
○

8. Which of these shapes is a cylinder?

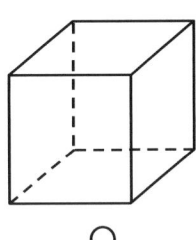
○

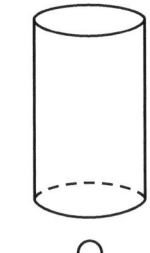
○

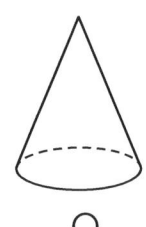
○

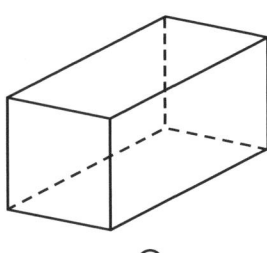
○

GO ON

9. Which shape has parts that are halves?

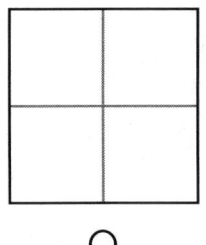 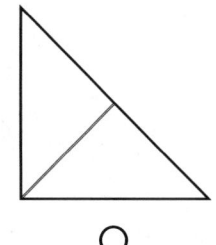

○   ○

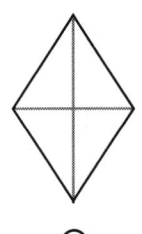 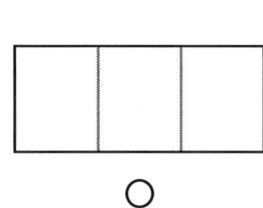

○   ○

10. Which shape shows thirds?

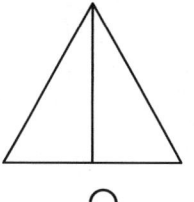 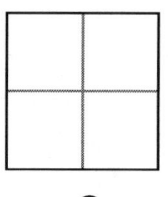

○   ○

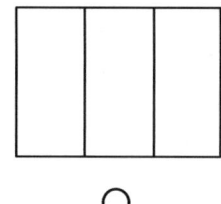 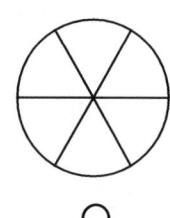

○   ○

11. Which sentence does **not** describe a rectangular prism?

○ A rectangular prism has 16 vertices.

○ A rectangular prism has 12 edges.

○ A rectangular prism has 6 faces.

○ At least two faces of a rectangular prism are rectangles.

12. Which shape shows 4 equal parts?

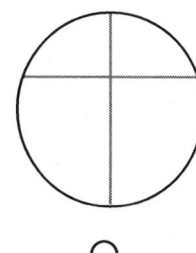 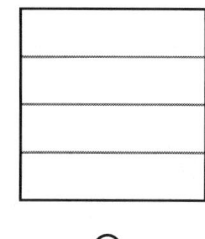

○   ○

 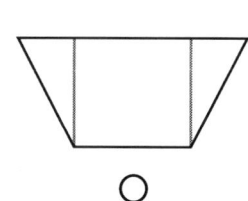

○   ○

GO ON ▶

13. Which names a shape with 6 sides and 6 vertices?

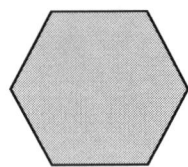

○ hexagon

○ pentagon

○ quadrilateral

○ triangle

14. How many sides does this quadrilateral have?

○ 1

○ 2

○ 3

○ 4

15. Which of these shapes has more than 5 angles?

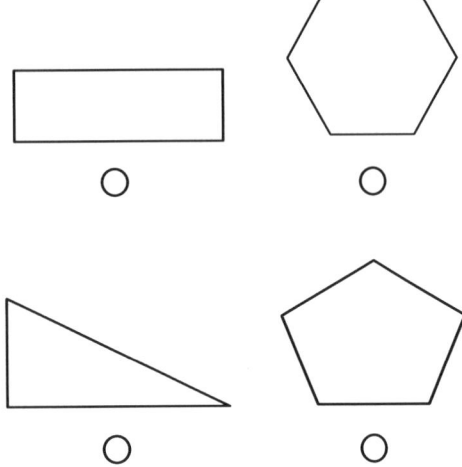

○   ○

○   ○

16. Theo used square tiles to cover this rectangle. How many square tiles did he use to cover the rectangle?

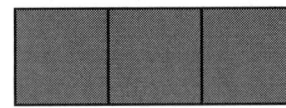

○ 4

○ 3

○ 2

○ 1

GO ON ➡

17. How many angles does this shape have?

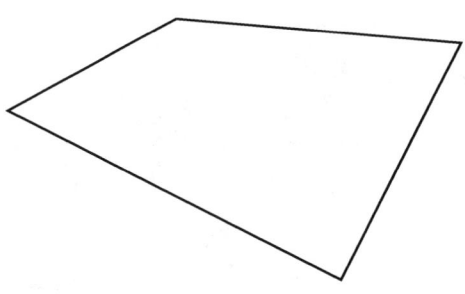

○ 3

○ 4

○ 5

○ 6

18. Paul cuts a sheet of paper into thirds like this.

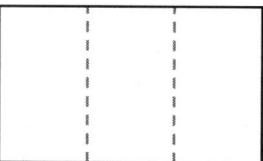

Which shows another way to cut the paper into thirds?

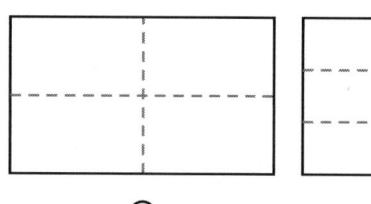

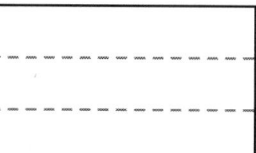

○   ○

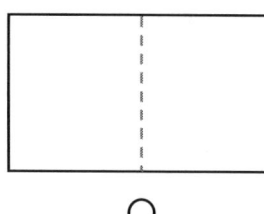

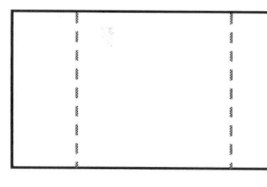

○   ○

19. Which object is shaped like a sphere?

○   ○

○   ○

20. Which object is shaped like a rectangular prism?

○   ○

   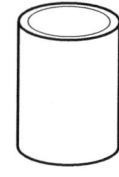

○   ○

GO ON ➡

Name _____

21. Which shape has parts that are thirds?

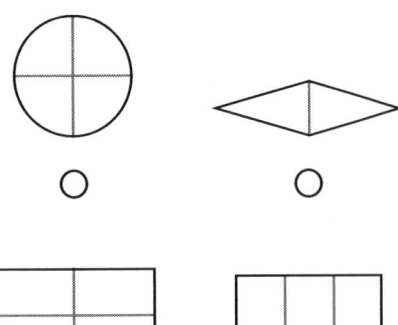

○   ○

○   ○

22. Which shows a half of the shape shaded?

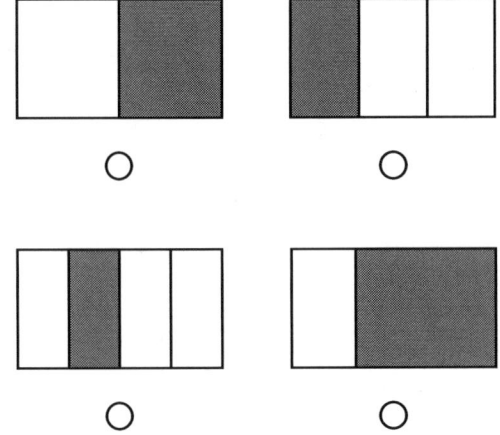

○   ○

○   ○

23. How many vertices does a rectangular prism have?

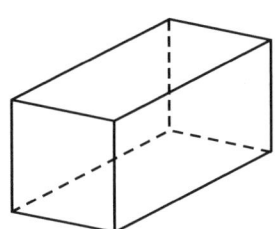

○ 8

○ 6

○ 5

○ 4

24. Which shape shows halves?

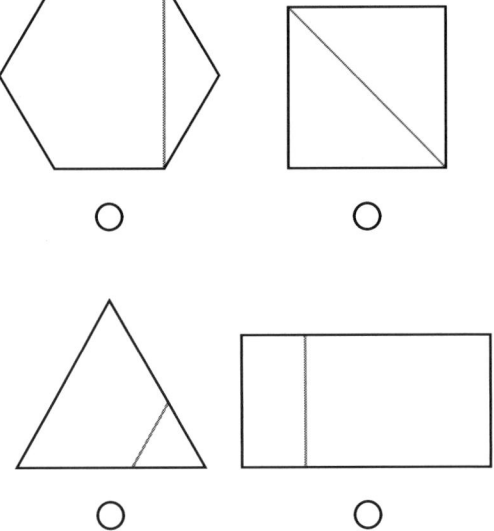

○   ○

○   ○

GO ON

25. Gracie wants to cover the rectangle with gray tiles. Explain how you would estimate the number of gray tiles she would need to cover the rectangle. What is your estimate?

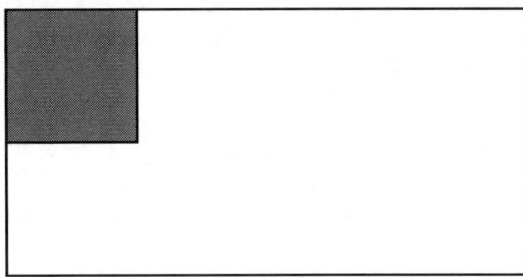

Answer _____

_____

26. Hector makes two equal sandwiches. Draw to show two different ways he can cut the sandwiches. How many equal parts is each sandwich made up of?

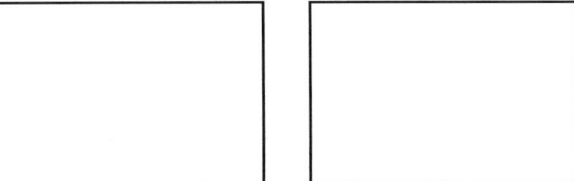

Answer _____

GO ON ▶

27. Draw lines to show fourths. How do you know the parts are fourths?

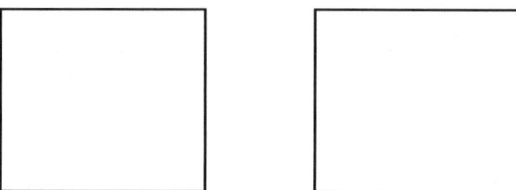

Answer _____

_____

---

28. Mason drew 2 two-dimensional shapes that had 8 angles in all.

PART A

Draw the shapes Mason could have drawn.

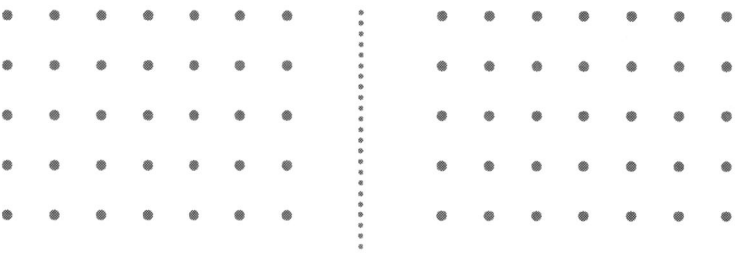

PART B

What are the names of the shapes?

Answer _____

Child's Name _____ Date _____

Prerequisite Skills Inventory

Item	Standard	Common Error	Personal Math Trainer
1	1.NBT.B.2b	May miscount the number of tens and ones	1.NBT.B.2b
2	1.NBT.B.2b	May confuse the tens place and the ones place	1.NBT.B.2b
3	1.NBT.B.2b	May draw the incorrect number of tens or ones	1.NBT.B.2b
4	1.NBT.B.2a	May group the objects incorrectly	1.NBT.B.2a
5	1.NBT.B.2a	May not understand that 10 ones are equal to 1 ten	1.NBT.B.2a
6	1.NBT.B.3	May confuse the symbols $<$ and $>$	1.NBT.B.3
7, 9	1.OA.C.6	May subtract incorrectly	1.OA.C.6
8, 10	1.OA.B.3	May add incorrectly	1.OA.B.3
11	1.OA.C.6	May not recognize related facts	1.OA.C.6
12	1.OA.C.6	May not realize how addition and subtraction are related	1.OA.C.6
13	1.OA.C.6	May not understand how to use the strategy *doubles plus one*	1.OA.C.6
14	1.OA.C.6	May not understand how to use the strategy *doubles plus one*	1.OA.C.6
15	1.OA.B.3	May add incorrectly	1.OA.B.3
16	1.OA.C.6	May not understand how to use the strategy *make a ten* to subtract	1.OA.C.6
17	1.NBT.C.6	May subtract multiples of 10 incorrectly	1.NBT.C.6
18	1.OA.B.3	May not recognize that they can combine $4 + 6$ to make a ten	1.OA.B.3

Child's Name _____ Date _____

Prerequisite Skills Inventory

Item		Common Error	Personal Math Trainer
19	1.NBT.C.4	May forget to regroup.	1.NBT.C.4
20	1.NBT.C.4	May not understand how to count on multiples of ten	1.NBT.C.4
21	1.MD.B.3	May not write the time correctly	1.MD.B.3
22	1.MD.B.3	May transpose the minute and hour hand	1.MD.B.3
23	1.MD.B.3	May draw clock hands incorrectly	1.MD.B.3
24	1.MD.C.4	May incorrectly count the data points in a category	1.MD.C.4
25	1.MD.C.4	May incorrectly count the total number of data points	1.MD.C.4
26	1.MD.C.4	May not understand how to compare quantities shown on a graph	1.MD.C.4
27, 28	1.MD.A.2	May not measure length correctly using nonstandard units	1.MD.A.2
29	1.MD.A.1	May not understand how to order objects by length using the terms *shortest* and *longest*	1.MD.A.1
30	1.MD.A.1	May not understand how to order lengths using indirect measures	1.MD.A.1
31	1.G.A.2	May have difficulty combining three-dimensional shapes into a composite figure	1.G.A.2
32	1.G.A.2	May have difficulty combining two-dimensional shapes into a composite figure	1.G.A.2
33	1.G.A.3	May not be able to identify the number of equal shares	1.G.A.3

Child's Name _____ Date _____

Beginning-of-Year/Middle-of-Year/End-of-Year Test

Item	Lesson	Standard	Common Error	Intervene with	Personal Math Trainer
1	3.5	2.OA.B.2	May not understand the term *related fact*	R—3.5	2.OA.2
2	3.9	2.OA.A.1	May use an incorrect number sentence to solve	R—3.9	2.OA.1
3	3.4	2.OA.B.2	May not add three addends correctly	R—3.4	2.OA.2
4	6.8	2.NBT.B.7	May not reduce the number in the hundreds column after regrouping	R—6.8	2.NBT.7
5	6.3	2.NBT.B.7	May not regroup correctly when adding the ones or tens	R—6.3	2.NBT.7
6	6.10	2.NBT.B.7	May not regroup correctly when there is a 0 in the tens	R—6.10	2.NBT.7
7	8.4	2.MD.A.1	May not line up the edge of the ruler when measuring	R—8.4	2.MD.1
8	8.9	2.MD.D.9	May have difficulty reading a line plot	R—8.9	2.MD.9
9	8.7	2.MD.A.3	May have difficulty estimating length in feet	R—8.7	2.MD.3
10	8.8	2.MD.A.1	May not understand the purposes of different measuring tools	R—8.8	2.MD.1
11	1.1	2.OA.C.3	May not understand the meaning of *even* and *odd*	R—1.1	2.OA.3
12	1.3	2.NBT.A.3	May not know the value of a digit in the ones or tens place	R—1.3	2.NBT.3
13	1.5	2.NBT.A.3	May not understand that a number can be written in different ways	R—1.5	2.NBT.3
14	1.9	2.NBT.A.2	May not understand how to count by 10s.	R—1.9	2.NBT.2
15	11.1	2.G.A.1	May not be able to identify three-dimensional shapes	R—11.1	2.G.1
16	11.4	2.G.A.1	May not understand properties of shapes.	R—11.4	2.G.1
17	11.5	2.G.A.1	May not understand how to sort shapes according to the number of sides and vertices	R—11.5	2.G.1

Key: R—Reteach

Child's Name _____ Date _____

Beginning-of-Year/Middle-of-Year/End-of-Year Test

Item	Lesson	Standard	Common Error	Intervene with	Personal Math Trainer
18	11.9	2.G.A.3	May not be able to identify a half, a third, or a fourth of a shape	**R**—11.9	2.G.3
19	4.10	2.OA.A.1	May find a difference instead of a sum	**R**—4.10	2.OA.1
20	4.11	2.NBT.B.6	May forget to add the third addend	**R**—4.11	2.NBT.6
21	4.9	2.NBT.B.5	May add incorrectly	**R**—4.9	2.NBT.5
22	4.7	2.NBT.B.5	May add incorrectly	**R**—4.7	2.NBT.5
23	10.2	2.MD.D.10	May misread the picture graph	**R**—10.2	2.MD.10
24	10.3	2.MD.D.10	May not understand how to complete a row of a picture graph	**R**—10.3	2.MD.10
25	10.1	2.MD.D.10	May not know that there are 5 tallies in each bundle	**R**—10.1	2.MD.10
26	10.4	2.MD.D.10	May misread the bar graph	**R**—10.4	2.MD.10
27	2.5	2.NBT.A.1	May not correctly identify the place value of the digits	**R**—2.5	2.NBT.1
28	2.7	2.NBT.A.3	May not recognize a number in expanded form	**R**—2.7	2.NBT.3
29	2.10	2.NBT.B.8	May not continue the pattern correctly	**R**—2.10	2.NBT.8
30	2.12	2.NBT.A.4	May not know how to use the $<$, $>$, and $=$ symbols	**R**—2.12	2.NBT.4
31	7.2	2.MD.C.8	May not be able to determine the value of a collection of coins	**R**—7.2	2.MD.8
32	7.5	2.MD.C.8	May not be able to identify coins that have a value of one dollar	**R**—7.5	2.MD.8
33	7.11	2.MD.C.7	May not understand A.M. and P.M.	**R**—7.11	2.MD.7
34	5.1	2.NBT.B.5	May break apart the ones incorrectly	**R**—5.1	2.NBT.5

Key: R—Reteach

Child's Name _____ Date _____

Beginning-of-Year/Middle-of-Year/End-of-Year Test

Item	Lesson	Standard	Common Error	Intervene with	Personal Math Trainer
35	5.10	2.OA.A.1	May not understand how to write a number sentence to represent the problem	R—5.10	2.OA.1
36	5.11	2.OA.A.1	May forget to complete all the steps to solve the problem	R—5.11	2.OA.1
37	5.5	2.NBT.B.5	May not subtract correctly	R—5.5	2.NBT.5
38	9.5	2.MD.A.2	May not understand the relationship between a centimeter and a meter	R—9.5	2.MD.2
39	9.3	2.MD.A.1	May not line up the end of the object with the 0 mark on the centimeter ruler	R—9.3	2.MD.1
40	9.7	2.MD.A.4	May perform the wrong operation when solving a problem about comparing lengths	R—9.7	2.MD.4
41	1.1	2.OA.C.3	May not understand the meaning of *even* and *odd*	R—1.1	2.OA.3
42	3.5	2.OA.A.1	May not add correctly	R—3.5	2.OA.1
43	6.5	2.NBT.B.7	May not add correctly	R—6.5	2.NBT.7
44	10.4	2.MD.D.10	May not read the bar graph correctly	R—10.4	2.MD.10
45	10.5	2.MD.D.10	May not draw the bar graph correctly	R—10.5	2.MD.10

Key: R—Reteach

Chapter 1 Test

Item	Lesson	Standard	Content Focus	Intervene With	Personal Math Trainer
19–21	1.1	2.OA.C.3	Classify numbers as even or odd.	R—1.1	2.OA.3
1, 2, 25	1.2	2.OA.C.3	Represent an even number.	R—1.2	2.OA.3
22–24	1.3	2.NBT.A.3	Identify the value of a digit in a 2-digit number.	R—1.3	2.NBT.3
11, 12, 27	1.9	2.NBT.A.2	Count by 10s.	R—1.9	2.NBT.2
3, 4	1.8	2.NBT.A.2	Count by 2s and 5s.	R—1.8	2.NBT.2
5–7, 28	1.4	2.NBT.A.3	Represent a 2-digit number with a drawing and describe in different forms.	R—1.4	2.NBT.3
13–15, 26	1.7	2.NBT.A.3	Use understanding of place value to solve problems.	R—1.7	2.NBT.3
16–18	1.6	2.NBT.A.3	Use understanding of place value to solve problems.	R—1.6	2.NBT.3
8–10	1.5	2.NBT.A.1	Write 2-digit numbers in word form, expanded form, and standard form.	R—1.5	2.NBT.1

Key: R—Reteach

Child's Name _____ Date _____

Chapter 2 Test

Item	Lesson	Standard	Content Focus	Intervene With	Personal Math Trainer
13, 14	2.1	2.NBT.A.1a 2.NBT.A.1b	Identify 10 tens as equivalent to 100.	R—2.1	2.NBT.1.a, 2.NBT.1.b
1, 2	2.2	2.NBT.A.1	Use groups of tens to solve problems with 3-digit numbers.	R—2.2	2.NBT.1
3, 4	2.9	2.NBT.B.8	Identify 10 more, 100 less.	R—2.9	2.NBT.8
17, 18	2.10	2.NBT.B.8	Use place value to identify and extend counting patterns.	R—2.10	2.NBT.8
21, 22	2.12	2.NBT.A.4	Compare 3-digit numbers using >, =, and <.	R—2.12	2.NBT.4
5, 27	2.4	2.NBT.A.3	Write 3-digit numbers in word form and expanded form.	R—2.4	2.NBT.3
6, 11, 12	2.7	2.NBT.A.3	Write 3-digit numbers in expanded and standard form.	R—2.7	2.NBT.3
23, 24, 25	2.3	2.NBT.A.1	Use place value to identify the values of digits.	R—2.3	2.NBT.1
15, 16, 26	2.8	2.NBT.A.3	Use a model to represent 3-digit numbers.	R—2.8	2.NBT.3
7, 8, 28	2.11	2.NBT.A.4	Use a model to solve problems using number comparisons.	R—2.11	2.NBT.4
9, 10	2.5	2.NBT.A.1	Use place to identify the values of digits.	R—2.5	2.NBT.1
19, 20	2.6	2.NBT.A.3	Write a 3-digit number in word form.	R—2.6	2.NBT.3

Key: R—Reteach

Chapter 3 Test

Item	Lesson	Standard	Content Focus	Intervene With	Personal Math Trainer
7, 8, 19	3.4	2.OA.B.2	Add 3 addends.	R—3.4	2.OA.2
4, 16	3.1	2.OA.B.2	Identify doubles facts.	R—3.1	2.OA.2
3, 15	3.7	2.OA.B.2	Subtract using a ten.	R—3.7	2.OA.2
6, 18	3.3	2.OA.B.2	Add and model addition using a ten.	R—3.3	2.OA.2
12, 24	3.11	2.OA.C.4	Find number of objects in an array using repeated addition.	R—3.11	2.OA.4
5, 17, 25	3.10	2.OA.C.4	Represent number of objects in equal groups.	R—3.10	2.OA.4
10, 21, 26	3.5	2.OA.B.2	Represent subtraction problem using a drawing and a number sentence.	R—3.5	2.OA.2
1, 13, 28	3.2	2.OA.B.2	Represent addition problem using a number sentence.	R—3.2	2.OA.2
2, 14, 27	3.6	2.OA.B.2	Identify correct subtraction facts.	R—3.6	2.OA.2
9, 20	3.9	2.OA.A.1	Represent subtraction problem using a number sentence.	R—3.9	2.OA.1
11, 22, 23	3.8	2.NBT.B.5	Use bar models to represent a variety of addition and subtraction situations.	R—3.8	2.NBT.5

Key: R—Reteach

Chapter 4 Test

Item	Lesson	Standard	Content Focus	Intervene With	Personal Math Trainer
23, 24	4.10	2.OA.A.1	Use a model and number sentence to solve an addition problem.	R—4.10	2.OA.1
3, 4, 20, 28	4.11	2.NBT.B.6	Add 3 numbers.	R—4.11	2.NBT.6
9, 10	4.6	2.NBT.B.5	Add 2-digit numbers.	R—4.6	2.NBT.5
21, 22, 25	4.5	2.NBT.B.6	Model and record 2-digit addition.	R—4.5	2.NBT.6
5, 6, 26	4.3	2.NBT.B.5	Add 2-digit numbers using mental math.	R—4.3	2.NBT.5
19, 20, 27	4.9	2.OA.A.1	Add 2-digit numbers.	R—4.9	2.OA.1
11, 12, 28	4.12	2.NBT.B.6	Add 4 numbers.	R—4.12	2.NBT.6
13, 14	4.7	2.NBT.B.5	Decide whether a sum is greater than or less than 100.	R—4.7	2.NBT.5
17, 18	4.1	2.NBT.B.6	Find equivalent ways to write a sum.	R—4.1	2.NBT.6
1, 2	4.2	2.NBT.B.5	Use compensation to develop flexible thinking for 2-digit addition.	R—4.2	2.NBT.5
7, 8	4.4	2.NBT.B.6	Model 2-digit addition with regrouping.	R—4.4	2.NBT.6
15, 16	4.8	2.NBT.B.6	Rewrite horizontal addition problems vertically in the standard algorithm format.	R—4.8	2.NBT.6

Key: R—Reteach

Child's Name _____ Date _____

Chapter 5 Test

Item	Lesson	Standard	Content Focus	Intervene With	Personal Math Trainer
6, 19	5.5	2.NBT.B.5	Determine whether regrouping is necessary when subtracting.	**R**—5.5	2.NBT.5
4, 16	5.8	2.NBT.B.5	Use a number line to add to find a difference.	**R**—5.8	2.NBT.5
9, 24, 28	5.9	2.OA.A.1	Use a bar model to solve a subtraction problem.	**R**—5.9	2.OA.1
3, 15	5.1	2.NBT.B.5	Break apart ones to subtract.	**R**—5.1	2.NBT.5
8, 21, 25	5.2	2.NBT.B.5	Break apart tens and ones to subtract.	**R**—5.2	2.NBT.5
2, 14	5.7	2.NBT.B.5	Rewrite and subtract.	**R**—5.7	2.NBT.5
10, 11, 22	5.11	2.OA.A.1	Complete bar models to solve a multistep subtraction problem.	**R**—5.11	2.OA.1
7, 20, 27	5.4	2.NBT.B.5	Record subtraction with regrouping.	**R**—5.4	2.NBT.5
1, 13, 26	5.3	2.NBT.B.5	Model regrouping in subtraction.	**R**—5.3	2.NBT.5
12, 23	5.10	2.OA.A.1	Write an equation to solve a subtraction problem.	**R**—5.10	2.OA.1
5, 17, 18	5.6	2.NBT.B.5	Practice 2-digit subtraction with and without regrouping.	**R**—5.6	2.NBT.5

Key: R—Reteach

Chapter 6 Test

Item	Lesson	Standard	Content Focus	Intervene With	Personal Math Trainer
7, 8, 16	6.3	2.NBT.B.7	Regroup ones to add.	R—6.3	2.NBT.7
10, 21, 22	6.6	2.NBT.B.7	Subtract 3-digit numbers without regrouping.	R—6.6	2.NBT.7
6, 18, 28	6.2	2.NBT.B.7	Break apart 3-digit addends.	R—6.2	2.NBT.7
5, 17, 25	6.1	2.NBT.B.7	Draw to represent 3-digit addition.	R—6.1	2.NBT.7
11, 23, 26	6.9	2.NBT.B.7	Regroup hundreds and tens to subtract.	R—6.9	2.NBT.7
3, 27	6.8	2.NBT.B.7	Regroup hundreds to subtract.	R—6.8	2.NBT.7
9, 19, 20	6.5	2.NBT.B.7	Regroup ones and tens to add.	R—6.5	2.NBT.7
4, 14, 15	6.4	2.NBT.B.7	Record 3-digit addition using the standard algorithm with possible regrouping of tens.	R—6.4	2.NBT.7
1, 2, 13	6.7	2.NBT.B.7	Record 3-digit subtraction using the standard algorithm with possible regrouping of tens.	R—6.7	2.NBT.7
12, 24	6.10	2.NBT.B.7	Record subtraction using the standard algorithm when there are zeros in the minuend.	R—6.10	2.NBT.7

Key: R—Reteach

Chapter 7 Test

Item	Lesson	Standard	Content Focus	Intervene With	Personal Math Trainer
23	7.7	2.MD.C.8	Select combinations of bills and coins with a given value.	R—7.7	2.MD.8
12, 24, 26	7.11	2.MD.C.7	Tell time from a clock as A.M. or P.M. based on the problem scenario.	R—7.11	2.MD.7
7, 27	7.4	2.MD.C.8	Show an amount using coins.	R—7.4	2.MD.8
11, 21, 25	7.5	2.MD.C.8	Count a collection of coins and compare to $1.00.	R—7.5	2.MD.8
3, 4, 15	7.9	2.MD.C.7	Tell time to the nearest 5 minutes.	R—7.9	2.MD.7
9, 19	7.10	2.MD.C.7	Tell time as minutes after an hour.	R—7.10	2.MD.7
5, 22	7.6	2.MD.C.8	Count a collection of a bill and coins with a total greater than $1.00.	R—7.6	2.MD.8
8, 17, 18, 28	7.2	2.MD.C.8	Count a collection of coins.	R—7.2	2.MD.8
1, 2, 13, 14	7.8	2.MD.C.7	Tell time to the half hour.	R—7.8	2.MD.7
6, 16	7.1	2.MD.C.8	Count a collection of coins.	R—7.1	2.MD.8
10, 20	7.3	2.MD.C.8	Order coins in a collection by value and then find the total value.	R—7.3	2.MD.8

Key: R—Reteach

Child's Name _____ Date _____

Chapter 8 Test

Item	Lesson	Standard	Content Focus	Intervene With	Personal Math Trainer
4, 15, 23, 25	8.8	2.MD.A.1	Choose a tool and explain.	R—8.8	2.MD.1
6, 17, 24, 26	8.5	2.NBT.B.5, 2.NBT.B.6	Relate addition to length and use a number line diagram.	R—8.5	2.MD.5, 2.MD.6
8, 9, 19	8.4	2.MD.A.2	Use a ruler to measure an object.	R—8.4	2.MD.2
5, 16, 20	8.1	2.MD.A.1	Measure length with an inch model.	R—8.1	2.MD.1
1, 2, 12, 13, 26	8.9	2.MD.D.9	Use a line plot and explain how it will change with data changes.	R—8.9	2.MD.9
3, 14	8.6	2.MD.A.2	Select inches or feet as the correct units for given measures.	R—8.6	2.MD.2
7, 18	8.3	2.MD.A.3	Estimate length using an inch model.	R—8.3	2.MD.3
10	8.7	2.MD.A.3	Estimate length in feet.	R—8.7	2.MD.3
11, 21, 22	8.2	2.MD.A.3	Make an inch ruler and use it to measure the lengths of objects.	R—8.2	2.MD.3

Key: R—Reteach

Child's Name _____ Date _____

Chapter 9 Test

Item	Lesson	Standard	Content Focus	Intervene With	Personal Math Trainer
2, 3, 12	9.1	2.MD.A.1	Measure length using a centimeter model.	**R**—9.1	2.MD.1
7, 8, 10, 17, 20	9.2	2.MD.A.3	Estimate length in centimeters.	**R**—9.2	2.MD.3
5, 14, 15, 21–23	9.4	2.MD.A.4	Relate addition to length and use a number line diagram.	**R**—9.4	2.MD.4
1	9.5	2.MD.A.2	Select centimeters or meters as the correct unit for given measures.	**R**—9.5	2.MD.1
4, 13	9.6	2.MD.A.3	Estimate length in meters.	**R**—9.6	2.MD.3
6, 11, 16	9.7	2.MD.A.4	Measure and compare lengths of two objects.	**R**—9.7	2.MD.4
9, 18, 19, 23	9.3	2.MD.A.1	Measure length to the nearest centimeter.	**R**—9.3	2.MD.1

Key: R—Reteach

Chapter 10 Test

Item	Lesson	Standard	Content Focus	Intervene With	Personal Math Trainer
9–12, 21–24	10.1	2.MD.D.10	Make a tally chart.	**R**—10.1	2.MD.10
1, 2, 14, 27	10.5	2.MD.D.10	Make and interpret a bar graph.	**R**—10.5	2.MD.10
3, 4, 15, 16	10.4	2.MD.D.10	Read and interpret a bar graph.	**R**—10.4	2.MD.10
7, 8, 19, 20, 25	10.3	2.MD.D.10	Complete a picture graph.	**R**—10.3	2.MD.10
5, 6, 17, 18, 25, 28	10.2	2.MD.D.10	Read and interpret a picture graph.	**R**—10.2	2.MD.10
26	10.6	2.MD.D.10	Solve problems involving data by using the strategy *make a graph*.	**R**—10.6	2.MD.10

Key: R—Reteach

Chapter 11 Test

Item	Lesson	Standard	Content Focus	Intervene With	Personal Math Trainer
7, 8, 19, 20	11.1	2.G.A.1	Match objects and three-dimensional shapes.	R—11.1	2.G.1
2, 11, 23	11.2	2.G.A.1	Identify attributes of a rectangular prism.	R—11.2	2.G.1
12, 24, 26, 27	11.8	2.G.A.3	Draw to show equal parts of a two-dimensional shape.	R—11.8	2.G.3
6, 18	11.10	2.G.A.3	Draw halves, thirds, and fourths.	R—11.10	2.G.3
9, 21	11.7	2.G.A.2	Identify and name equal parts.	R—11.7	2.G.2
1, 13, 14, 28	11.3	2.G.A.1	Determine the number of cubes in a rectangular prism.	R—11.3	2.G.1
5, 17, 28	11.4	2.G.A.1	Count sides of two-dimensional shapes to solve a problem.	R—11.4	2.G.1
3, 15	11.5	2.G.A.1	Draw two-dimensional shapes with a given number of angles.	R—11.5	2.G.1
10, 22	11.9	2.G.A.3	Identify shapes divided into thirds.	R—11.9	2.G.3
4, 16, 25	11.6	2.G.A.1	Partition rectangles into equal-size squares and find the total number of these squares.	R—11.6	2.G.1

Key: R—Reteach

Correlations

	Lesson Objectives	Test/Item Numbers
1.1	Classify numbers up to 20 as even or odd.	Chapter 1 Test: 19–21 Beginning/Middle/End-of-Year Test: 11, 41
1.2	Write equations with equal addends to represent even numbers.	Chapter 1 Test: 1, 2, 25
1.3	Use place value to describe the values of digits in 2-digit numbers.	Chapter 1 Test: 22–24 Beginning/Middle/End-of-Year Test: 12
1.4	Write 2-digit numbers in expanded form.	Chapter 1 Test: 5–7, 28
1.5	Write 2-digit numbers in word form, expanded form, and standard form.	Chapter 1 Test: 8–10 Beginning/Middle/End-of-Year Test: 13
1.6	Apply place value concepts to find equivalent representations of numbers.	Chapter 1 Test: 16–18
1.7	Solve problems by finding different combinations of tens and ones to represent 2-digit numbers using the strategy *find a pattern*.	Chapter 1 Test: 13–15, 26
1.8	Extend counting sequences within 100, counting by 1s, 5s, and 10s.	Chapter 1 Test: 3, 4
1.9	Extend counting sequences within 1,000, counting by 1s, 5s, 10s, and 100s.	Chapter 1 Test: 11, 12, 27 Beginning/Middle/End-of-Year Test: 14
2.1	Understand that each group of 10 tens is equivalent to 1 hundred.	Chapter 2 Test: 13, 14
2.2	Write 3-digit numbers that are represented by groups of tens.	Chapter 2 Test: 1, 2
2.3	Use concrete and pictorial models to represent 3-digit numbers.	Chapter 2 Test: 23, 24, 25
2.4	Apply place value concepts to write 3-digit numbers that are represented by pictorial models.	Chapter 2 Test: 5, 27
2.5	Use place value to describe the values of digits in numbers to 1,000.	Chapter 2 Test: 9, 10 Beginning/Middle/End-of-Year Test: 27
2.6	Read and write 3-digit numbers in word form.	Chapter 2 Test: 19, 20
2.7	Write 3-digit numbers in expanded form and in standard form.	Chapter 2 Test: 6, 11, 12 Beginning/Middle/End-of-Year Test: 28
2.8	Apply place value concepts to find equivalent representations of numbers.	Chapter 2 Test: 15, 16, 26
2.9	Identify 10 more, 10 less, 100 more, or 100 less than a given number.	Chapter 2 Test: 3, 4
2.10	Extend number patterns by counting on by tens or hundreds.	Chapter 2 Test: 17, 18 Beginning/Middle/End-of-Year Test: 29

	Lesson Objectives	Test/Item Numbers
2.11	Solve problems involving number comparisons by using the strategy *make a model*.	Chapter 2 Test: 7, 8, 28
2.12	Compare 3-digit numbers using the >, =, and < symbols.	Chapter 2 Test: 21, 22 Beginning/Middle/End-of-Year Test: 30
3.1	Use doubles facts as a strategy for finding sums for near doubles facts.	Chapter 3 Test: 4, 16
3.2	Recall sums for basic facts using properties and strategies.	Chapter 3 Test: 1, 13, 28
3.3	Recall sums for addition facts using the make a ten strategy.	Chapter 3 Test: 6, 18
3.4	Find sums of three addends by applying the Commutative and Associative Properties of Addition.	Chapter 3 Test: 7, 8, 19 Beginning/Middle/End-of-Year Test: 3
3.5	Use the inverse relationship of addition and subtraction to recall basic facts.	Chapter 3 Test: 10, 21, 26 Beginning/Middle/End-of-Year Test: 1, 42
3.6	Recall differences for basic facts using mental strategies.	Chapter 3 Test: 2, 14, 27
3.7	Find differences on a number line to develop the mental strategy of decomposing to simplify facts.	Chapter 3 Test: 3, 15
3.8	Use bar models to represent a variety of addition and subtraction situations.	Chapter 3 Test: 11, 22, 23
3.9	Write equations to represent and solve a variety of addition and subtraction situations.	Chapter 3 Test: 9, 20 Beginning/Middle/End-of-Year Test: 2
3.10	Solve problems involving equal groups by using the strategy *act it out*.	Chapter 3 Test: 5, 17, 25
3.11	Write equations using repeated addition to find the total number of objects in arrays.	Chapter 3 Test: 12, 24
4.1	Find a sum by breaking apart a 1-digit addend to make a 2-digit addend a multiple of 10.	Chapter 4 Test: 17, 18
4.2	Use compensation to develop flexible thinking for 2-digit addition.	Chapter 4 Test: 1, 2
4.3	Apply place-value concepts when using a break-apart strategy for 2-digit addition.	Chapter 4 Test: 5, 6, 26
4.4	Model 2-digit addition with regrouping.	Chapter 4 Test: 7, 8
4.5	Draw quick pictures and record 2-digit addition using the standard algorithm.	Chapter 4 Test: 21, 22, 25
4.6	Record 2-digit addition using the standard algorithm.	Chapter 4 Test: 9, 10
4.7	Practice 2-digit addition with and without regrouping.	Chapter 4 Test: 13, 14 Beginning/Middle/End-of-Year Test: 22

Lesson Objectives		Test/Item Numbers
4.8	Rewrite horizontal addition problems vertically in the standard algorithm format.	Chapter 4 Test: 15, 16
4.9	Solve problems involving 2-digit addition by using the strategy *draw a diagram*.	Chapter 4 Test: 19, 20, 27 Beginning/Middle/End-of-Year Test: 21
4.10	Represent addition situations with number sentences using a symbol for the unknown number.	Chapter 4 Test: 23, 24 Beginning/Middle/End-of-Year Test: 19
4.11	Find sums of three 2-digit numbers.	Chapter 4 Test: 3, 4, 20, 28 Beginning/Middle/End-of-Year Test: 20
4.12	Find sums of four 2-digit numbers.	Chapter 4 Test: 11, 12, 28
5.1	Break apart a 1-digit subtrahend to subtract it from a 2-digit number.	Chapter 5 Test: 3, 15 Beginning/Middle/End-of-Year Test: 34
5.2	Break apart a 2-digit subtrahend to subtract it from a 2-digit number.	Chapter 5 Test: 8, 21, 25
5.3	Model 2-digit subtraction with regrouping.	Chapter 5 Test: 1, 13, 26
5.4	Draw quick pictures and record 2-digit subtraction using the standard algorithm.	Chapter 5 Test: 7, 20, 27
5.5	Record 2-digit subtraction using the standard algorithm.	Chapter 5 Test: 6, 19 Beginning/Middle/End-of-Year Test: 37
5.6	Practice 2-digit subtraction with and without regrouping.	Chapter 5 Test: 5, 17, 18
5.7	Rewrite horizontal subtraction problems vertically in the standard algorithm format.	Chapter 5 Test: 2, 14
5.8	Use addition to find differences.	Chapter 5 Test: 4, 16
5.9	Solve problems involving 2-digit subtraction by using the strategy *draw a diagram*.	Chapter 5 Test: 9, 24, 28
5.10	Represent subtraction situations with number sentences using a symbol for the unknown number.	Chapter 5 Test: 12, 23 Beginning/Middle/End-of-Year Test: 35
5.11	Analyze word problems to determine what operations to use to solve multistep problems.	Chapter 5 Test: 10, 11, 22 Beginning/Middle/End-of-Year Test: 36
6.1	Draw quick pictures to represent 3-digit addition.	Chapter 6 Test: 5, 17, 25
6.2	Apply place value concepts when using a break apart strategy for 3-digit addition.	Chapter 6 Test: 6, 18, 28
6.3	Record 3-digit addition using the standard algorithm with possible regrouping of ones.	Chapter 6 Test: 7, 8, 16 Beginning/Middle/End-of-Year Test: 5
6.4	Record 3-digit addition using the standard algorithm with possible regrouping of tens.	Chapter 6 Test: 4, 14, 15

Lesson Objectives		Test/Item Numbers
6.5	Record 3-digit addition using the standard algorithm with possible regrouping of both ones and tens.	Chapter 6 Test: 9, 19, 20 Beginning/Middle/End-of-Year Test: 43
6.6	Solve problems involving 3-digit subtraction by using the strategy *make a model*.	Chapter 6 Test: 10, 21, 22
6.7	Record 3-digit subtraction using the standard algorithm with possible regrouping of tens.	Chapter 6 Test: 1, 2, 13
6.8	Record 3-digit subtraction using the standard algorithm with possible regrouping of hundreds.	Chapter 6 Test: 3, 27 Beginning/Middle/End-of-Year Test: 4
6.9	Record 3-digit subtraction using the standard algorithm with possible regrouping of both hundreds and tens.	Chapter 6 Test: 11, 23, 26
6.10	Record subtraction using the standard algorithm when there are zeros in the minuend.	Chapter 6 Test: 12, 24 Beginning/Middle/End-of-Year Test: 6
7.1	Find the total values of collections of dimes, nickels, and pennies.	Chapter 7 Test: 6, 16
7.2	Find the total values of collections of quarters, dimes, nickels, and pennies.	Chapter 7 Test: 8, 17, 18, 28 Beginning/Middle/End-of-Year Test: 31
7.3	Order coins in a collection by value and then find the total value.	Chapter 7 Test: 10, 20
7.4	Represent money amounts less than a dollar using two different combinations of coins.	Chapter 7 Test: 7, 27
7.5	Show one dollar in a variety of ways.	Chapter 7 Test: 11, 21, 25 Beginning/Middle/End-of-Year Test: 32
7.6	Find and record the total value for money amounts greater than $1.	Chapter 7 Test: 5, 22
7.7	Solve word problems involving money by using the strategy *act it out*.	Chapter 7 Test: 23
7.8	Tell and write time to the hour and half hour.	Chapter 7 Test: 1, 2, 13, 14
7.9	Tell and write time to the nearest five minutes.	Chapter 7 Test: 3, 4, 15
7.10	Practice telling time to the nearest five minutes.	Chapter 7 Test: 9, 19
7.11	Tell and write time using a.m. and p.m.	Chapter 7 Test: 12, 24, 26 Beginning/Middle/End-of-Year Test: 33
8.1	Use concrete models to measure the lengths of objects in inches.	Chapter 8 Test: 5, 16, 20
8.2	Make an inch ruler and use it to measure the lengths of objects.	Chapter 8 Test: 11, 21, 22
8.3	Estimate the lengths of objects by mentally partitioning the lengths into inches.	Chapter 8 Test: 7, 18

	Lesson Objectives	Test/Item Numbers
8.4	Measure the lengths of objects to the nearest inch using an inch ruler.	Chapter 8 Test: 8, 9, 19 Beginning/Middle/End-of-Year Test: 7
8.5	Solve addition and subtraction problems involving the lengths of objects by using the strategy *draw a diagram*.	Chapter 8 Test: 6, 17, 24, 26
8.6	Measure the lengths of objects in both inches and feet to explore the inverse relationship between size and number of units.	Chapter 8 Test: 3, 14
8.7	Estimate the lengths of objects in feet.	Chapter 8 Test: 10 Beginning/Middle/End-of-Year Test: 9
8.8	Select appropriate tools for measuring different lengths.	Chapter 8 Test: 4, 15, 23, 25 Beginning/Middle/End-of-Year Test: 10
8.9	Measure the lengths of objects and use a line plot to display the measurement data.	Chapter 8 Test: 1, 2, 12, 13, 26 Beginning/Middle/End-of-Year Test: 8
9.1	Use a concrete model to measure the lengths of objects in centimeters.	Chapter 9 Test: 2, 3, 12
9.2	Estimate lengths of objects in centimeters by comparing them to known lengths.	Chapter 9 Test: 7, 8, 10, 17, 20
9.3	Measure lengths of objects to the nearest centimeter using a centimeter ruler.	Chapter 9 Test: 9, 18, 19, 23 Beginning/Middle/End-of-Year Test: 39
9.4	Solve problems involving adding and subtracting lengths by using the strategy *draw a diagram*.	Chapter 9 Test: 5, 14, 15, 21–23
9.5	Measure the lengths of objects in both centimeters and meters to explore the inverse relationship between size and number of units.	Chapter 9 Test: 1 Beginning/Middle/End-of-Year Test: 38
9.6	Estimate the lengths of objects in meters.	Chapter 9 Test: 4, 13
9.7	Measure and then find the difference in the lengths of two objects.	Chapter 9 Test: 6, 11, 16 Beginning/Middle/End-of-Year Test: 40
10.1	Collect data in a survey and record that data in a tally chart.	Chapter 10 Test: 9–12, 21–24 Beginning/Middle/End-of-Year Test: 25
10.2	Interpret data in picture graphs and use that information to solve problems.	Chapter 10 Test: 5, 6, 17, 18, 25, 28 Beginning/Middle/End-of-Year Test: 23
10.3	Make picture graphs to represent data.	Chapter 10 Test: 7, 8, 19, 20, 25 Beginning/Middle/End-of-Year Test: 24
10.4	Interpret data in bar graphs and use that information to solve problems.	Chapter 10 Test: 3, 4, 15, 16 Beginning/Middle/End-of-Year Test: 26, 44
10.5	Make bar graphs to represent data.	Chapter 10 Test: 1, 2, 14, 27 Beginning/Middle/End-of-Year Test: 44
10.6	Solve problems involving data by using the strategy *make a graph*.	Chapter 10 Test: 26
11.1	Identify three-dimensional shapes.	Chapter 11 Test: 7, 8, 19, 20 Beginning/Middle/End-of-Year Test: 15

Lesson Objectives		Test/Item Numbers
11.2	Identify and describe three-dimensional shapes according to the number of faces, edges, and vertices.	Chapter 11 Test: 2, 11, 23
11.3	Name 3-, 4-, 5-, and 6-sided shapes according to the number of sides and vertices.	Chapter 11 Test: 1, 13, 14, 28
11.4	Identify angles in two-dimensional shapes.	Chapter 11 Test: 5, 17, 28 Beginning/Middle/End-of-Year Test: 16
11.5	Sort two-dimensional shapes according to their attributes.	Chapter 11 Test: 3, 15 Beginning/Middle/End-of-Year Test: 17
11.6	Partition rectangles into equal-size squares and find the total number of these squares.	Chapter 11 Test: 4, 16, 25
11.7	Identify and name equal parts of circles and rectangles as halves, thirds, or fourths.	Chapter 11 Test: 9, 21
11.8	Partition shapes to show halves, thirds, or fourths.	Chapter 11 Test: 12, 24, 26, 27
11.9	Identify and describe one equal part as a half of, a third of, or a fourth of a whole.	Chapter 11 Test: 10, 22 Beginning/Middle/End-of-Year Test: 18
11.10	Solve problems involving wholes divided into equal shares by using the strategy *draw a diagram*.	Chapter 11 Test: 6, 18